# *the* LEADER'S MINDSET

## Praise for
## *the* LEADER'S MINDSET

*"Want to be a better leader? Read* The Leader's Mindset *and then DO WHAT IT TELLS YOU TO DO! You won't regret it."*
— **Chester Elton**, *New York Times*–bestselling author of *All In*

*"Terence Mauri assembles the strands of leadership DNA that are the key to success — both for yourself and for the people you lead."*
— **Jeff Haden**, contributing editor, *Inc.* magazine

*"Insightful leadership wisdom for aspiring leaders distilled into practical, actionable advice."*
— **Doug Conant**, chairman, Kellogg Executive Leadership Institute, and former CEO, Campbell Soup, Inc.

*"Extraordinary leaders are not born, they're made. This book offers a deep-dive into some of the most practical advice on how to become one."*
— **Emilia Lahti**, Aalto University School of Science and Technology, and founder of the Sisu Lab

*"The Leader's Mindset helps you to find and clarify your purpose, coupling smart prose with in-depth, international examples covering the spectrums of business, philosophy, and psychology. Terence Mauri illustrates how to stay nimble, yet decisive in our rapidly changing world: a fine read for anyone looking to take their leadership skills to the next level."*
— **MITx Entrepreneurship Team**, Massachusetts Institute of Technology

*"The difference between the best leaders and the rest is not who they know or even what they know but how they think. This book goes with the practical precision to the cerebellum of leadership."*
— **Octavius Black**, CEO, Mind Gym

*"A game changer."*
— **Joel Brown**, CEO and founder of Addicted to Success

*"The Leader's Mindset unlocks the gates to exponentially better leadership. Packed with enlightening stories and grounded in research, Terence Mauri has written a book for anyone who wants to up their game."*
— **Kevin Kruse**, *New York Times*–bestselling author of *Employee Engagement 2.0*

*"As a leader, it takes courage and boldness to change the world, and it's not always easy – but it's the most fulfilling of any choices you can make. With Terence Mauri's expert advice, you now know how."*
— **Hans Balmaekers**, CEO and founder of Saam

*"The Leader's Mindset tells you clearly how to harness the mindset of a disruptive leader."*
— **Gordon Tredgold**, CEO and founder of Leadership Principles and Visiting Professor, Staffordshire University

*"Before reading* The Leader's Mindset, *I thought I was stretching myself. But Terence Mauri showed me how I was holding myself back and what to do to really go big, to truly open up the possibilities for success.* The Leader's Mindset *shows you why some leaders are able to be true visionaries, how to identify the needs of the future before they exist, and what to do to lead your company there. In* The Leader's Mindset *Mauri outlines a path that's easy to follow and inspiring to think about, with great examples of success."*
— **Josh Davis, PhD**, author of *Two Awesome Hours: Science-Based Strategies to Harness Your Best Time and Get Your Most Important Work Done*

"*Terence Mauri unfolds masterfully the core aspects of leadership in our current times. With an outstanding empirical approach, this book will help you to understand the importance of the leader's mindset for business success.*"

— **Jésus Blanco**, co-founder and CEO of Linktia

*the*
# LEADER'S MINDSET

## How to Win
## IN THE AGE OF
## DISRUPTION

## TERENCE MAURI

New York

# *the* LEADER'S MINDSET
## How to Win **IN THE AGE OF DISRUTION**

Published in New York, New York, by Morgan James Publishing. Morgan James and The Entrepreneurial Publisher are trademarks of Morgan James, LLC.
www.MorganJamesPublishing.com

The Morgan James Speakers Group can bring authors to your live event. For more information or to book an event visit The Morgan James Speakers Group at www.TheMorganJamesSpeakersGroup.com.

**Shelfie**

A **free** eBook edition is available with the purchase of this print book.

CLEARLY PRINT YOUR NAME ABOVE IN UPPER CASE

**Instructions to claim your free eBook edition:**
1. Download the Shelfie app for Android or iOS
2. Write your name in **UPPER CASE** above
3. Use the Shelfie app to submit a photo
4. Download your eBook to any device

ISBN 978-1-63047-878-0 paperback
ISBN 978-1-63047-879-7 eBook
ISBN 978-1-63047-914-5 hardcover
Library of Congress Control Number:
2015920595

**Cover Design by:**
Rachel Lopez
www.r2cdesign.com

**Interior Design by:**
Bonnie Bushman
The Whole Caboodle Graphic Design

In an effort to support local communities and raise awareness and funds, Morgan James Publishing donates a percentage of all book sales for the life of each book to Habitat for Humanity Peninsula and Greater Williamsburg.

Get involved today, visit
www.MorganJamesBuilds.com

**Habitat for Humanity®**
Peninsula and
Greater Williamsburg
Building Partner

*To my family*

# CONTENTS

# CHAPTER 1

# UNLOCKING THE LEADER'S MINDSET

*"If you don't innovate fast, disrupt your industry, disrupt yourself, you'll be left behind."*
— **John Chambers**, CEO of Cisco,
speaking at the World Economic Forum, 2015

Let's play a quick game. Why are the numbers 480, 168, and 960 significant?

First, 480 is the number of minutes in an eight-hour day. That's not much when you consider the avalanche of social media demands, meetings, and other battles for your attention. Recently, a CEO confessed to me: "If I get interrupted just once every five minutes, that's ninety-six interruptions a day. It's almost impossible to focus. My whole day is spent reacting to the latest emergency. Something has to change."

Things got so bad that his wife responded to the chaos by throwing his cell phone in the washing machine. I do not recommend this as a coping strategy.

As for 168, this is the number of hours in a week. Today's breakneck work pace has greatly impacted how we think—for much of our 168 hours, we're struggling to focus on what really matters. According to a recent global survey by LinkedIn,[1] the online business network, a whopping 89 percent of people say they don't achieve their daily goals. We're distracted, our brains are tired, and we're having more accidents. I've witnessed this phenomenon firsthand. Once, I saw a person walk straight into a fountain because they were looking down at their cell phone. We now live in a "look down" world. A new study commissioned by Nokia, the communications and technology company, showed that the average person checks their phone 150 times a day and gets anxious after only ten minutes away from it.[2] Some people are even known to feel their phone vibrate when it's switched off!

If you paddle too hard, the boat capsizes. In a world of ever increasing overload, we must become more adept at cutting through the barrage of noise and battles for our attention. Our mindset is one of constant distraction. Psychologist Herbert A. Simon writes: "Information consumes the attention of its recipients. Hence a wealth of information creates a poverty of attention."[3]

New research by YouGov, the market research organization, shows that only one in seven Americans wakes up feeling fresh every day of the week and a whopping one in four wakes up mentally exhausted on four or more days.[4] The Japanese have a word for this busy state, *karoshi*, which literally translates as "death from overwork." This is a fate we must avoid at all costs.

This all leads to the final and most humbling number—960. Nine hundred sixty months is the amount of time we may have on this earth if we're lucky. The number translates to eighty years of age—29,200 days to be exact! When I discovered I'd already used up more than 500 of my 960 months, my mouth fell open in shock. Sadly, we spend so much of our precious time committing to a job we don't believe in or a career that leaves us feeling like a shadow of our former selves. Knowing the number of months we have left on this planet can help us clarify what really matters. It's time to upgrade your mindset for the age of disruption. Something sets it apart, makes it stand out, and gives it unique capabilities.

I call it the leader's mindset. Do I have your attention now? Good.

## MINDSET IN MOTION

Jan Koum and Brian Acton are the founders of WhatsApp, the world's most famous messaging app. Its mission is to "empower people through technology and communication, no matter who they are, or where they live."[5]

Their remarkable journey is a hallmark of courage, willpower, and relentless determination. In a *Guardian* newspaper interview, Acton describes the relationship as "yin and yang." He says: "I'm the naïve optimist, he's more paranoid. I pay attention to bills and taxes, he [Koum] pays attention to our product."[6]

Koum was born in a rural village outside of Kiev, Ukraine. At the age of sixteen, during much political strife and instability, his family made the agonizing decision to flee their country and move to Mountain View, California. Koum's father could not join them and was left behind. Koum told one interviewer: "I grew up in a society where everything you did was eavesdropped on, recorded, snitched on."[7] Koum's difficult childhood experience under Soviet surveillance undoubtedly influenced the design of the WhatsApp messaging service.

Koum and Acton are no strangers to failure and rejection. In the summer of 2009, Acton was looking for a job. For more than eleven years, the Stanford computer science graduate had been working at Yahoo, the social networking business, in various engineering roles.

He used Twitter to share his news.[8]

**7:06 PM, 20 MAY 2009**

Networking with recruiters, venture capitalists, playing ultimate Frisbee.

**8:39 PM, 23 May 2009**

Got denied by Twitter HQ. That's OK. Would have been a long commute.

**8:14 PM, 3 Aug 2009**

Facebook turned me down. It was a great opportunity to connect with some fantastic people. Looking forward to life's next adventure.

Whatever you choose to believe, life is anything but predictable. Just five years later, in a miraculous twist of fate, Facebook bought WhatsApp for $19 billion.[9]

To put the deal in perspective, at the time of purchase, the hotel chain Marriott International had over 120,000 staff, a twenty-two-year history, and a market cap of over $15.4 billion.[10] WhatsApp has only fifty-five employees, although I hear they are hiring.

How did this unlikely pair become two of the most successful entrepreneurs on the planet? The answer: they had harnessed the leader's mindset by having the brains to disrupt the technology industry, and the guts to disrupt themselves.

## 10X THINKING

Astro Teller is a British entrepreneur, scientist, and thinker who is widely credited as one of the pioneers of 10X thinking (10X). He heads up Google X, a futuristic lab responsible for hyper-ambitious projects such as Google Glass, Project Loon, a balloon-powered Wi-Fi network, and the infamous Google self-driving car. According to legend, his business card describes him as "Captain of Moon Shots".

His story inspired me to embark on a journey to unlock the anatomy of a leader's mindset at many of the world's most exciting companies, from young startups to global giants.

Along the way, I uncovered some surprising insights about how the smartest leaders' brains are wired differently than those of other business people. In an interview with *Wired* magazine, Teller explains the power of 10X thinking: "There are tests that you can apply to see if you're thinking big enough. The easiest one, the mantra that we use at Google X, is ten times rather than ten percent better, you tend to work from where you are: if I ask you to make a car that goes 50 miles a gallon, you can just retool the engine you already have. But if I tell you it has to run on a gallon of gas for 500 miles, you're going to have to start over. That causes you to approach the problem so differently that weirdly, counter-intuitively, it's often easier to make something ten times better—because perspective-shifting is just that much more powerful than hard work and resources being thrown at problems via traditional, well-tried paths."[11]

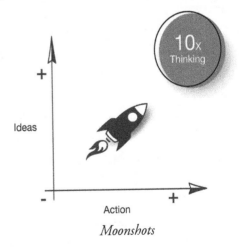

*Moonshots*

Imagine leading your organization up to ten times better than you do today or increasing your team's success tenfold. 10X thinking is the golden thread that links all great leaders and is at the core of how to win in the age of disruption.

My challenge had been set. I wanted to answer the question: "What must you 10X in order to unlock the leader's mindset?"

## INNOVATION WAY

On a recent visit to Silicon Valley, it occurred to me that while it's a place, it should mostly be seen as a mindset.

A mindset is a leader's way of thinking: it's their beliefs, attitudes, choices and assumptions that affect how leaders view the world and their work. Silicon Valley borders Cupertino, home of Apple, Inc., the world's most valuable company, and Mountain View, the home of Google's Googleplex headquarters. One road is aptly named Innovation Way. Leaders radiate optimism and genuinely care about what you're doing. I call it passionate curiosity. Instead of asking, "What do you do?" they'll ask: "How can I help and who do you know?" There's a freedom to be yourself: nobody is waiting for approval or permission. It's impossible to not feel hugely invigorated by the energy, ideas, and sheer determination to make things happen. This type of environment can have a big impact on the way you think, perhaps unlike anywhere else on the planet.

It's no accident that Silicon Valley is a household name today all around the world. Its herculean rise is in large part due to 10X thinking from the "father of Silicon Valley" Frederick Terman[12] to, in more recent times, Y Combinator cofounders Paul Graham and Sam Altman.

These leaders have thrown out the rulebook on leadership: the leader's mindset demands you to rethink assumptions about what is possible. Even if you achieve only 60 percent of a 10X goal, you will have grown your team and your business, and probably learned some important things about yourself along the way. I believe 10X thinking is central to a leader's mindset and is about pushing people to think bigger, breaking out of those little boxes that we get trapped in. It's about reimagining the future and asking if we started again today what would be different? We tend to associate 10X just with new ideas but it's possible to apply it to anything in your organization, from improving culture to how you scale more rapidly. I came to the conclusion that you can 10X any part of your leadership role when you choose the right mindset. For example, now I don't limit myself to just one mentor. I have multiple mentors. For me, this is the essence of a leader's mindset. It stops you from thinking small.

## LEADERSHIP REWRITTEN

In 2016, the number of startup "unicorns", small, fast-growing technology firms with valuations of more than $1 billion, is at record levels.[13] The big guys know that survival requires leading differently and continually finding new ways of doing things that the competition doesn't. CEOs are sweating in boardrooms up and down the country as young upstarts force them to completely rethink how they run their companies. Many are virtually asset-free: Uber, the biggest taxi company, does not own cars; Airbnb, the biggest provider of accommodations, does not own hotels; and Google, the world's most popular media company, does not own content.

Leadership is undergoing a seismic and long-overdue shift.

In many companies, there's a chronic leadership gap: teams are being overmanaged and underled. To progress, we must all become leaders of ourselves; this means we must make change happen and become a lifelong learner of leadership. Michael Raddatz, at fashion company Bottega Veneta, tells me: "In such a flat world where numerous opportunities arise, our challenge is to seize the ones that will allow you to become 'you'. Leadership books always mention the importance of getting out of your comfort zone to reach new heights, both personal and professional. But how does one differentiate challenges from dangers? At the end of the day, you are the one and only person who can make the decision. These decisions have an impact on your mindset and your future. So I'm quite confident in saying that the leaders out there that inspire the world are, before anything, great self-leaders; they have seized the right opportunities to be (or become) themselves and shine."

In *The Leader's Mindset*, you will learn about "moonshots", the revolutionary ideas that have the greatest impact on your leadership results. Unless you spend every hour of the day awake, it's a bad strategy to try to do everything. You must know what *not* to do. Clear thinking helps a leader remain focused on the "critical few". The "critical few" is another way of saying the 80/20 rule. This clever rule of thumb says that 20 percent of anything drives 80 percent of outcomes. For example, 20 percent of your leadership actions will produce 80 percent of your results. Can you think of any others? Now that you know about this, you'll start seeing it everywhere. With limited time and resources, you must identify the critical few leadership actions that will give you the most leverage. This means thinking, acting, and leading in

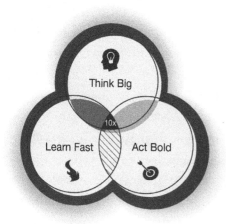

*The Leader's Mindset*

a way that gets results and taps into the biggest sources of potential in yourself, and your organization.

There are three action-oriented mindsets you must 10X to win in the age of disruption. They are practical shortcuts for simplifying how we think, how we act, and, ultimately, how we lead.

## 1. Think Big Mindset (Future Shaper)

When was the last time you set a challenge for yourself that pushed you to deliver more than you thought was humanly possible? Most leaders think about how they can lead better by 10 percent or 20 percent, not by a factor of ten. The leader's mindset is hardwired to think bigger and brighter, whether it's wiping out malaria in the next ten years (the Bill and Melinda Gates Foundation) or making space tourism a reality (Richard Branson and Elon Musk). These leaders have an eye on the future and can spot an unmet opportunity quickly before others. They're not afraid of change and enjoy bucking the norm. They are future shapers.

You don't have to be a CEO or run a startup to think big. It's about taking control of your vision rather than someone else hiring you to fulfill theirs. Get started, have a clear destination, fail fast, test ideas lightly and often, and know that those who shape the future hold two beliefs: (1) problems can't be solved with yesterday's thinking, and (2) you have the resources to achieve your goals.

Shaping the future starts with finding your "why", your leadership purpose. Leaders spend a lot of time on their mission statements. I see them on the walls of corridors and boardrooms everywhere, but most aren't living up to their aspirations or their purpose. This observation is backed up by Gallup, Inc., the leading management consultancy, whose research shows that "only slightly more than one-third of U.S. workers strongly agree that their company's mission or purpose makes them feel their job is important."[14] This represents an enormous untapped opportunity for leaders everywhere, according to *Fast Company* writer Robert Safian: "Mission is the essential strategic tool that allows them to filter the modern barrage of stimuli, to motivate and engage those around them, and to find new and innovative ways to solve the world's problems. Their experiences show the critical advantages of building mission in your career and your business. Companies that find and then live by their mission often discover that it becomes their greatest competitive advantage."[15]

## 2. Act Bold Mindset (Risk Taker)

What is it that enables leaders to persevere through seemingly insurmountable challenges that at first seem to exceed our limits? Make a list of leaders you admire and who have made a difference in the world. They could be living or dead. The chances are they all have one outstanding quality in common: they are bold.

A bold mindset excels at speed, creativity, and decisive action. They are risk takers. It's not the only factor that drives success, but perhaps it is one of the most important in the age of overload. We all face the twin problems of deciding what to do and what to tune out. Creativity enables leaders to imagine different solutions to a problem and can help you "cut through the noise and focus on the signal," as high profile entrepreneur Elon Musk describes it. If you want to make an impact, you need to act boldly, especially when the going gets tough.

Adversity is a natural part of the leadership journey. I have discovered that at the core of a leader's mindset is an attitude, rooted in an ancient Nordic belief system called *sisu*. *Sisu* refers to "extraordinary determination, courage and resoluteness in the face of extreme stress or adversity."[16] Every leader I have studied overcame battles that seemed insurmountable at the time and yet they did not give up.

At some point we will all open the door and face our own Mount Everest. It could be finding the strength to tackle a failure or bouncing back from a personal tragedy or setback.

Mine came when I was seven years old—a driver sped out of control, mounted a curb, and crashed into a shop where my family and I were standing. We nearly lost our lives. Ever since that day I've understood that part of the power of *sisu* lies in its hope-inducing nature. Hope is the sparkplug of all action, according to the world's leading researcher on hope, Dr. Shane Lopez.[17] It's in that split moment that you have a choice either to accept defeat or push past barriers. As the late British prime minister Winston Churchill once implored, "never, ever, ever give up."

### 3. Learn Fast Mindset (Knowledge Seeker)

Today, business is inherently more complex than it has ever been. Yves Morieux, senior partner at strategy consultancy Boston Consulting Group (BCG), has developed an index to show how business complexity has increased sixfold during the past sixty years alone. And organizational complexity (number of procedures, structures, processes, systems, vertical layers, and decision approvals) increased by a factor of thirty-five.[18] To learn fast, you must be interested in people and ideas, not just yourself. "Be savvy, flexible, learn from mistakes and collaborate with well-connected people," writes Shane Snow, the author of *Smartcuts: How Hackers, Innovators, and Icons Accelerate Success*.[19] Those who learn fast build diverse knowledge pools and tap into the wisdom of mentors to raise their game. They are knowledge seekers for whom questioning, experimenting, and adapting is the norm.

### FROM IDEA TO REALITY

Many of the ideas in this book come from my keynote talk "The Leader's Mindset". The talk helps leaders to think bigger, "see" things that are normally ignored, and find value in what's missing. More than 5,000 people have attended, ranging from Fortune 500 leaders to founders of fledgling startups.

As a business educator and mentor, my work constantly takes me around the world. I've met leaders from all walks of life including a Duke, and spoken at or attended some of the best conferences on the planet, including TechCrunch's Disrupt, GrowCo, Digital Life by Design, and TED. These encounters changed my life and provided me a rich insight into what it takes to think and act like a leader.

When you tap into the leader's mindset, you'll see more:

- **Significance.** Millennials are the first generation where a one-hundred-year life span and multiple careers will be common. They'll have to learn, unlearn, and relearn as some industries die and others become completely automated. Smiley Poswolsky writes in his book *The Quarter-Life Breakthrough*: "Far from me me me generation, ours is the Purpose Generation, a group who refuses to settle, because we know how great our impact is when we find work we care about."[20] Those who find their calling and match it with their strengths are happier and more successful. The leader's mindset begins with zero compromise on purpose. It demands that you believe in what you're doing and that your contribution is essential to the world.

- **Courage.** "There is no instinct like that of the heart," wrote Lord Byron.[21] The best leaders shake up the status quo, deal with failure, and make tough decisions fast. Every big 10,000-person company wants to think like a startup: small companies have "can do" cultures, habits and ways of working that give them an edge over their much larger and cumbersome rivals. The leaders of tomorrow will have to find the intellectual courage to change their business models two or even three times in order to remain viable. The bad news is that they're probably not going to learn this new mindset at business school.

- **Ideas.** TED (www.ted.com) is the global community devoted to spreading ideas, usually in the form of influential eighteen-minute talks. Its mission is to promote "ideas worth spreading". New ideas that change the world matched with talent and energy are at the core of what leaders do best. The head of MIT's Media Lab, Joi Ito said in a *Wired* interview: "The biggest change that Moore's Law and the internet have caused is the decrease in the cost of innovation, and the decrease in the cost of collaboration and distribution. The amount of money, and the amount of permission that you need to create an idea has decreased dramatically, whether it's Wikipedia, Yahoo, Facebook, or Google. They didn't have to ask for permission, and didn't even need to raise money to do it. They just did it. That pushes innovation to the edges so you no longer need money, power and control to innovate."[22] Now you can prototype an idea and get it up and running faster than ever before.

When you tap into the leader's mindset, you'll see less:

- **SEP.** This stands for "somebody else's problem". It's endemic in many companies and is the opposite of the leader's mindset. You know the characters: blame throwers, energy suckers, silent assassins, and misery monsters that drag the whole team down. A SEP culture means avoidance: excuses, inertia, and lazy back covering. Like a disease that's airborne, SEP can contaminate a team, a company, and even you. The leader's mindset does more with less; the whole team must be resourceful in order to optimize the resources as far as they can and create a positive work environment. Everybody becomes a leader.

- **Wasted Talent.** A key, non-negotiable role of every leader is fueling the organization's growth by utilizing the best talent. One of the saddest truths for any organization is wasted talent—the moment when somebody mentally quits the job but continues to turn up at the office. For those with the leader's mindset, it's about return on intelligence. This means using a team's unique strengths to do great work and making a difference beyond chasing profit.

- **Fear.** Fear can cause flight-fight or freeze behaviors and a hasty retreat from your biggest dreams, goals, and plans. Leaders give up and therefore guarantee their fate but also condemn themselves to fear's closest cousin: regret. Fear takes many forms, including fear of failure, fear of the unknown, procrastination, and doubt. Most of the biggest battles you'll ever fight will be inside your own head: *I'm not ready. I might fail. It won't work.* Fear keeps your mindset locked in a state of helplessness and can stop you from reaching your goals.

## NEXT STEPS

*The Leader's Mindset* will help you to do great work and excel in a fast, volatile world. Every leader knows that they must disrupt the status quo or they'll risk becoming it; they must step into the unknown to create new things that have not been created before.

We must all take care to make the most of our 960 months. At best, many leaders are sleepwalking. We are the distracted generation, always stuck to our cell phone screens, our minds busy and exhausted from always being "on" 24/7.

You can choose to be a leader, a follower, or out of business. When you decide, something will happen at a cellular level: you will feel alive. The leader's mindset is not satisfied with just good enough. Being able to wake up excited in the morning to do meaningful work is the very foundation of personal wellbeing and happiness.

*The Leader's Mindset* is organized into four sections: "Think Big Mindset", "Act Bold Mindset", "Learn Fast Mindset", and a conclusion, "Final Thoughts, Hacks, and Shortcuts". Each section is useful on its own, but their convergence is the key to unlocking the leader's mindset within yourself and your organization. Remove one section and the journey slows down. Commit to all of them and change will begin to unfold.

# CHAPTER 2

# THINK BIG MINDSET (FUTURE SHAPER)

*"If you can clearly articulate the dream or the goal, start."*
— **Simon Sinek**, author of *Start with Why*

**To "Think Big" (Future Shaper):**
1. Put vision at the heart of your everyday actions.
2. Switch quickly between big picture and detail focus.
3. Understand leadership is about "we, not me".
4. Build a strong culture of purpose.
5. Be a Chief Entrepreneur Officer.

## FROM ZERO TO 10X

How do you take your vision from zero to 10X? Think of great leaders you admire and chances are they all think big. Pioneering *sisu* researcher and TEDx speaker Emilia Lahti writes: "All of the major developments of modern civilization have depended on a person or group of people's ability to prospect possible futures, and to be bold enough to dream and go where no one has gone before. It is about taking a leap of faith, and trusting that when the moment comes we are able keep up the practice, stand behind our vision and push through the obstacles."[23]

This is the first rule of the leader's mindset: build a clear vision of the future, scale rapidly, and be ready make some tough calls in order to reach the destination.

## THE MAGIC IS OUTSIDE OF YOUR COMFORT ZONE

Entrepreneur and inventor Elon Musk is a lionhearted leader with a strong stomach for risk. He revels in thinking big, from inventing an environmentally friendly car to making space travel a reality. Even among

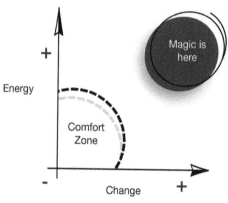

*Visionary Firepower*

fellow entrepreneurs, the scale of Musk's ambition sets him apart from most leaders who tackle the world's biggest problems. His one-hundred-hour work weeks and estimated $11 billion fortune make him the closest thing we have to the fictional superhero Tony Stark, aka Iron Man.[24] In a *Wired* interview, he says: "There's a tremendous bias against taking risks. Everyone is trying to optimize their ass-covering."[25] He's the CEO, chief technical officer, and chairman at three companies, all of which he founded: SpaceX, Tesla Motors, and Solar City. His passion for adventure has won fans the world over, with some calling him a "thrillionaire" who will one day have a planet named after him. They may be on to something. Born in Pretoria, South Africa, Musk is no stranger to hard work, revealing single-minded ambition from an early age. He has a vivid imagination, obsessive focus, and deep curiosity about the world and business in particular. He is brave not just in his words but his actions, and he uses failure in a systematic way for moving fast. He says: "We should not be afraid of doing something just because some amount of tragedy is likely to occur. If our forefathers had taken that approach, the United States wouldn't exist."[26]

At age twelve, Musk sold his first computer code for a game called Blastar for $500. A leader was born. Musk is no stranger to change. He understands that it is the outer edge of our comfort zone where the magic awaits. At seventeen he moved to Canada to avoid serving in the apartheid-backed South African Army. There he continued his studies, earning a bachelor of science in physics. At twenty-four, he made the life-changing decision to move to California to begin doctorate studies in applied physics at Stanford University, but after a few days he left the program to become an entrepreneur. And leaving paid off: Musk became a multimillionaire. While he was still in his twenties, he sold his first software company, Zip2, to Compaq for more than $300 million.[27]

Soon after, he set up his next venture, X.com, an online e-commerce payment company, which later merged with PayPal, the online payment company. Just three years later, in 2002, eBay acquired PayPal for more than $1.5 billion. Musk's trajectory has been truly remarkable.

The world needs more heroes like Musk. Now in his early forties, he is a role model for people around the world who want to change the world. It all begins with the right mindset. As a leader, that means instilling everybody with a purpose and providing meaningful work that gives pride. Musk says: "You have to have a very compelling goal for the company. If you put yourself in the shoes of someone who's talented at a world class level, they have to believe that there's potential for a great outcome and believe in the leader of the company, that you're the right guy to work with. That can be a difficult thing, especially if you're trying to attract people from other companies."[28]

Musk is someone who doesn't give up easily and excels at managing his inner critic. He says: "I think it is possible for ordinary people to choose to be extraordinary."[29] It's so easy to listen to the little man— that's the gremlin in your own head. Every day it tells you that you're not good enough or that idea will never work. Musk knows that the key to success is a willingness to bet on the future and learn fast, to adopt a leader's mindset. Switch off the little man or even put him on mute—remember, you're in control. At a commencement speech in 2012, Musk said: "Going from PayPal, I thought well, what are some of the other problems that are likely to most affect the future of humanity? Not from the perspective, 'what's the best way to make money,' which is okay, but, it was really 'what do I think is going to most affect the future of humanity?'"[30]

Musk also wants to solve California's legendary traffic problem. He has revealed plans for a futuristic transport system that would shuttle travelers from Los Angeles to San Francisco, a 380-mile journey, in less than thirty minutes. Dubbed the "Hyperloop", it would reach speeds of up to 760 mph (1,220 kmh). Hyperloop Transportation Technologies, Inc., has already convinced the best engineers around the world to volunteer their expertise to the new venture. Yes, it's not a typo: *volunteer*. *Wired* reported that "nearly all of them have day jobs at companies like Boeing, NASA, Yahoo, and Airbus. They're smart. And they're organized."[31]

Arguably, Tesla is Musk's most famous company to date. Inspired by Nikola Tesla, the nineteenth-century inventor who patented the first AC inductor, it is blazing a trail in the multitrillion-dollar automotive market. The flagship Model S is popular with many and can reach a jaw-dropping 60 mph in 3.1 seconds.

It's what some might call a head turner. Musk founded Tesla in 2003 with the audacious goal to rethink the entire automobile industry. Its mission is to "create the most compelling car company of the 21st century by driving the world's transition to electric vehicles." The best leaders have anticipation skills—the creative ability to scan the environment and spot opportunities before they go mainstream. Tesla's Model S has won fans around the world, including a stream of awards such as *Time* magazine's Best Inventions of the Year 2012 and the highest rating ever (99/100) by *Consumer Reports*.[32]

Musk is his own person, someone who's comfortable in his own skin. We can all learn from that. He comes from a foundation of deep humility. It's OK to be wrong. It's OK to fail. It doesn't make you a worthless human being. In an interview for CNN's Top 10 Thinkers, he says: "When starting out Tesla and SpaceX, in both cases, I thought the odds of success were less than 50%... So it's not as though I was convinced that it would all work. I thought, 'Well, it probably won't work, but it's worth a try because the outcome is important.'"[33] That level of self-honesty shows a leader who is prepared to play the long game. All of his projects have been high stakes—he could have easily lost his fortune ten times over.

Big ideas come from big thinkers. On April 15, 2015, Tesla announced its revolutionary new invention, Powerwall, which aims to take homes and offices around the world off the grid and into the future.

A hallmark of a leader's mindset is a desire to master the context rather than give in to it. It's about seeing and shaping the future sooner than the competition. Musk is a leader who is ready to dive in, knowing that the obstacles to success will be significant. This means using your brains to imagine a distinct future and then having the belief to back that vision up with laser-like focus and daily effort. Anything worthwhile in business or life will be difficult. These days, leaders expect too many shortcuts and when they hit a wall, too many of them give up immediately.

On starting a business, Musk says: "You encounter issues you didn't expect, step on landmines. It's bad. Years two to four or five are usually quite difficult. A friend has a saying—'it's eating glass and staring into the abyss.'"[34]

What future are you prepared to commit to? It's not easy to close the door and jump into the unknown, bringing your boldest self to your biggest challenges. I've confronted the same challenge when I moved from a rewarding and stable career in consultancy to becoming an entrepreneur and business mentor. Our default setting is to stay in familiar surroundings and accept defeat before even trying. How many times have you thought about a game-changing idea only to let it melt away like snow under the sun? This is known as the "zone of regret". Remember, the cost of trying anything in life will never be as painful as never knowing. Facebook chief operating officer Sheryl Sandberg said it best when she delivered a speech to a graduating class of Harvard Business School: "Get on a rocket ship. When companies are growing quickly and they are having a lot of impact, careers take care of themselves. And when companies aren't growing quickly or their missions don't matter as much, that's when stagnation and politics come in. If you're offered a seat on a rocket ship, don't ask what seat. Just get on."[35]

The take-home message here? Whatever you're doing you should be passionate about it. If you're not, then just say no.

## AN UNCERTAIN WORLD

Like Elon Musk, all leaders must get ahead in a VUCA world. This stands for volatility (rapid, large-scale change), uncertainty (unclear about present and future outcomes), complexity (many factors to consider with no single cause or solution), and ambiguity (lack of clarity on what events mean and the impact they have). Originally coined by the US military during the Cold War, VUCA is a useful framework for understanding the disruptive forces at work. These forces present tremendous risk but also tremendous opportunity. It feels like anything is possible. Just look at how China's Xiaomi went from zero in 2011 to become the world's fastest-growing tech startup with a valuation of more than $46 billion.[36]

VUCA is about rapid change and the unrelenting acceleration of technology. Japan is about to open the world's first hotel run by robots,

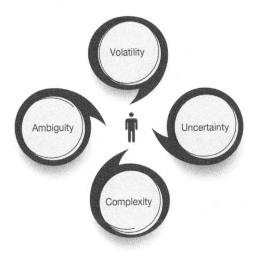

*Leading in a VUCA World*

and driverless cars are closer than you think. Carmakers Audi, BMW, and Mercedes are already testing models that will be hands-free, change lanes on their own, and park automatically.

It's now easier than ever before to fall behind and never catch up. The average life expectancy of Fortune 500 companies has fallen from seventy-five years in the 1930s to just fifteen years today.[37]

Many companies we know today simply won't exist in the future. In a popular feature, the *Huffington Post* outlined the disruptive forces of VUCA:

> When Apple launched their first iPhone in 2007, one of the comments from the CEO of Research in Motion (the company that created the Blackberry) was, "Why would anyone want to watch a video on a phone?" Obviously, he did not see the future. Failing to see the future, failing to understand the difference between hard trends (trends that will happen) and soft trends (trends that might happen), is what often causes companies to fall behind. With today's

rapid pace of technological change, falling behind can mean you may never catch up.[38]

Blockbuster, the video rental company, offers a timely lesson in underestimating the power of VUCA. At its height in the mid-nineties, it had over 60,000 stores and 9,000 employees; yet by September 2010, Blockbuster had filed for Chapter 11 bankruptcy.[39] The video rental industry had fundamentally shifted forever due to dramatic technological change. Now, it's easier and cheaper to rent a film online rather than to rent from a video store.

There are several strategies to remain curious and alert to the forces of VUCA. Companies must walk through the "valley of death" and overcome significant threats in order to survive: limited resources, risk, and little capital. First you must become an avid learner of leadership. Learn from good leaders and bad ones throughout your career and read books about leaders who you admire in history. The deep insights and lessons you can assimilate are priceless. Next, find a mentor and don't just settle for one. Aim for multiple mentors with different backgrounds who you can tap for ideas or advice. Most of all, get into the game—this means grab opportunities, break through comfort zones, and take the risk.

## THE CHILD TECHNOLOGY OFFICER

VUCA has affected my own life dramatically, too. Let me introduce you to the CTO. That's child technology officer to you and me. Most families have one. Usually the smallest and youngest member of the family, they become the go-to person for all technology issues. Pairing an iPad to the iPhone and navigating around social media is second nature to them. They're savvy, ask probing questions, and cope with change. In short, we can learn a lot from our children, who are highly adept at thriving in this hyper-connected world.

## RIPPLE INTELLIGENCE

Leaders must embrace a beginner's mindset of continual learning and curiosity. San Francisco's TechCrunch doesn't call its conference "Disrupt" for no reason. At the 2015 WED annual summit, researchers at Saïd Business School, part of Oxford University, in partnership with the executive search firm Heidrick & Struggles, released a new study titled "The CEO Report". More than 150 CEOs were interviewed to provide a deeper understanding of the most critical skills leaders must learn for the twenty-first century.

One of the core skills for a leader's mindset is cultivating a way of thinking called "ripple intelligence". Peter Tufano, writing in the *Financial Times*'s *Boldness in Business* magazine, says leaders who have honed ripple intelligence "appear to see around corners and connect new dots."[40]

Can you navigate different trends, changes, and contexts that can disrupt an industry or business, for better or worse? Ripple intelligence is "the ability to see the interactions of business contexts like ripples moving across a pond."[41] One of the

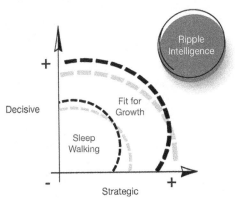

*Ripple Intelligence*

best ways to develop this intelligence is to step outside your normal orbit and have a point of view about the ideas, trends, and issues that keep you awake at night, as well as the ones that excite you. Done well, this can help you anticipate hidden opportunities and catch the next big wave before others do. As uncertainties multiply, so do the opportunities.

Here are four ways to build ripple intelligence, an essential trait for the leader's mindset.

### Innovation Jams

One of the biggest challenges any leader faces is becoming a victim of status quo bias. This happens when we become fixated with protecting the past rather than embracing new ideas and accepting the need to change. Innovation jams can make you smarter and more innovative, for example, by helping you pull ideas together or see problems from a fresh perspective. Steven Johnson, author of *Where Good Ideas Come From*, writes: "Good ideas boil down to a network of neurons within your brain. This network grows as it is exposed to different environments and different ways of thinking. As you learn and become educated, new networks are being formed. Creativity ultimately happens when you can take pieces of this network and combine them in a unique way."[42]

Companies such as IBM are famed for their twenty-four-hour innovation jams. Innovation jams cleverly gamify the workplace with twenty-four-hour competitions to attack the biggest challenges facing the business, and they bring teams together to look at new and better ways to get work done. As part of the activity, an "irritations inventory" is compiled to prioritize what's making employees' lives more difficult. As the clock ticks away, ideas must be generated using an agreed-upon framework. When teams are empowered to test an idea, it can be changed or scrapped early in the process. They get real-time feedback and learning on the go. The exercise helps avoid multimillion-dollar mistakes down the road, too.

Teams with game-changing ideas are invited to pitch their proposals to the company's board of directors. The winners receive funding and recognition for their contribution. Innovation jams are a useful platform for energizing teams and making people feel recognized and valued. Doug Conant, former CEO of Campbell Soup, advises: "It's unrealistic to expect extraordinary effort and performance without creating an environment where people feel extraordinarily valued."[43]

## Outside-in Thinkers

Outside thinkers from different fields (arts, science, technology) are invited inside companies to fire up imaginations and develop outside-in thinking skills—this is the ability to look objectively at your organization through the eyes of an outsider or competitor. One startup examines the Renaissance period, hoping to pick up insights for winning in the twenty-first century. Amy Cosper, editor of *Entrepreneur*, studied art history and writes: "Art is a good teacher. Its lessons are not solely of the canvas. Above all, this education sheds light on the importance of a renaissance—a rebirth of ideas and a celebration of new ways of seeing the world. I have no regrets. On paper, my degree is in art history; but to me, my expertise is in critical thought."[44]

Another company organizes improvisational leadership classes for its team to help it think on its feet more quickly. Improvisation boosts creativity and self-confidence, two vital qualities for thinking fast under pressure. It's about trusting your own instincts and being open-minded enough to try something different.

Time-poor leaders can use resources such as GetAbstract.com and Blinkist to strengthen their outside-in thinking. These new apps provide concise executive summaries of some of the world's most popular business books and ensure that you stay up to date with the latest trends. Whatever you decide, do something decisive to avoid the corrosive effects of an SEP mindset.

## Future-Proof Teams (FPT)

Inspired by the scenario planning work at Shell, the oil and gas company, the aim of future-proof teams is to explore plausible visions of the future in order to make better decisions today. As speed capital becomes a huge source of advantage for companies, it's critical that leaders build cultures that can adapt quickly. Led by the top team, they report back their research and findings on a quarterly basis in the form of a lively debate.

To improve the quality of the predictions, everyone must be brutally honest. It's OK to be wrong. They admit it and learn from it just as much as they enjoy being right. Apart from building up a talented pool of strategic thinkers, other advantages include team collaboration and a culture of candor. Everybody wins.

Think of future-proofing as if you're writing a narrative about your own personal leadership story. You start with the main plot of how your business evolved, and then think of different ways the plot might unfold. The outcomes of these scenarios range from favorable to highly unfavorable. Future-proof exercises assess how prepared you are as a leader to cope in a number of different scenarios. Like a stress test, these tools can help you grab opportunities and remain ahead of the curve.

## Hedgehogs and Foxes

> *The fox knows many things, but the hedgehog knows one big thing.*
> — **Archilochus**, 700 BC

How you think is as important as what you think, especially for growing a leader's mindset. Leaders must tap into different thinking styles to learn quickly and cope in a world of flux; for example, they must develop big-picture thinking versus detail thinking. The late Oxford University professor Isaiah Berlin, in his book *The Hedgehog and the Fox*, drew upon the ancient metaphor by Greek poet Archilochus to describe the two distinct cognitive styles that can help you build critical advantages into your leadership style.[45]

There's always a risk of oversimplification when it comes to matters of the mind. The key is to ensure that you adopt the right style for the right context. Hedgehogs are left-brain thinkers: operationally driven, detail oriented, logical, and process led. They are essential for running a tight ship. Bill Gates, the founder of Microsoft, is a stalwart hedgehog. You need hedgehogs to maintain high operational standards, compliance, and efficient rules and processes.

Foxes are right-brain thinkers: opportunity driven, led by ideas, and people-oriented. They pursue moonshots, the crazy ideas that might just work. Richard Branson, the charismatic entrepreneur, is a quintessential fox. Smart leaders use the best elements of both to stay ahead. For example, to get the creative edge, an idea is generated by a fox, but the hedgehog is equally critical for providing a framework to help evaluate the fox's right brain inspirations: are they realistic? What's the budget? Can they be implemented? What's the timeline?

To figure out if you are a hedgehog or a fox, place a check by each word from the list below that describes your thinking style the most at work. The category with the most checked words indicates your primary style.

**Hedgehogs**
- ❑ Operationally driven (for example, Nokia)
- ❑ Detail oriented
- ❑ Logical
- ❑ Risk averse
- ❑ Status quo defender
- ❑ Specialists
- ❑ Accurate
- ❑ Logical
- ❑ Slow
- ❑ Planners
-    Total: _____

**Foxes**
- ❑ Opportunity driven (for example, Google, Inc.)
- ❑ Big-picture oriented
- ❑ Strategic

- ❏ Abstract thinkers
- ❏ Innovation inspired
- ❏ Risk takers
- ❏ Change agents
- ❏ Speedy
- ❏ Ideas driven
- ❏ People oriented
- ❏ Entrepreneurial
  Total: _____

Nokia and Google are two global companies that offer useful lessons in the merits of each style. Nokia is one of Finland's most famous exports, with a rich history dating back to 1865, and its leadership is more operationally driven (the hedgehog style).[46] My first cell phone in the late 1990s was a heavy brick-sized Nokia with a battery that lasted days rather than hours. This was a time before app stores, Twitter, and instant messaging had taken off. I loved it. Nokia was the largest mobile handset maker in the world. It sold its billionth phone by 2005, and by 2007 was one of the world's top ten most valued brands (the same year that Apple launched its first iPhone).[47] At its peak, Nokia generated more than 4 percent of Finland's gross domestic product, and its market capitalization reached over $320 billion.[48]

In 2014 Microsoft acquired Nokia's once-mighty mobile division for $7.2 billion, leaving just 900 employees, a fraction of the 24,000-plus employed during the good times. Nokia's road to obscurity is far from unique (Kodak, Blackberry, and Motorola are other casualties). There are three crucial lessons for leaders to learn from Nokia's debacle.[49]

First, as an operationally driven organization, Nokia became a victim of its own huge success. I call it the comfort trap. When companies get big, they tend to become too comfortable doing the same thing, just making incremental change and defending the status quo rather than disrupting it. Those with a leader's mindset are first and foremost chief enablers of change and understand that you need to be a bit uncomfortable to stay relevant.

Second, Nokia lost its ability to anticipate the future. Again, this happens more with large bureaucratic companies that have been immensely successful but have forgotten to think like a startup and apply the very principles that won them success in the first place. As every surfer knows, catching a great wave requires 20:20 vision on the horizon ahead. As the wave approaches, the surfer must decide on his strategy and begin to paddle out at the right speed; paddle too slowly and the wave comes crashing down on you. It's the same for leaders. If you don't prepare for change and pivot quickly, it will be too late—you drown.

Third, Nokia underestimated the impact of new entrants, such as Apple and Samsung. Hedgehog leaders and by definition their companies do well in more stable operating environments but may struggle in a VUCA world in which every business must be in a perpetual state of renewal.

Google, Inc. (an opportunity-driven organization) has recently restructured itself into a new holding company called Alphabet, which will preside over a collection of companies (Google; its biggest subsidiary, Calico; Nest; Fiber; Ventures Capital; and the X Lab). We tend to think of Google primarily as a search business, but that's just one part of its portfolio, sitting alongside other products such as Chrome, Android, and driverless cars. Like Warren Buffett's Berkshire Hathaway or General Electric, Alphabet will invest in groundbreaking new ideas to drive the next big growth areas.[50]

Samsung Electronics is another opportunity-driven organization and one of the world's biggest smartphone manufacturers. It's also the world's largest television manufacturer and holds prominent market positions in a number of industries from memory chips to tablet computers. Like Nokia, it has a prestigious heritage—it was founded in 1938—but conversely it has been brave enough to disrupt itself faster in order to stay ahead of the competition. Change is part of the DNA of everything it does, and for this reason the company continues to grow, despite competition from startups as well as behemoths such as Apple, Microsoft, and Google. At Samsung, they change everything except their partners and kids.

The need for ripple intelligence isn't going to go away anytime soon. As some business models fail, opportunity-driven leaders will be needed for finding original new ways to solve our most pressing challenges. That's not to say that operationally driven leaders have become redundant. Far from it, a successful company needs a healthy balance of both styles to prosper.

## FIND YOUR LEADERSHIP PURPOSE

In 2014, Amazon founder Jeff Bezos was named number one in *Harvard Business Review*'s annual "Best Performing CEOs in the World" study.[51] In a *Wired* interview, Bezos outlined how he plays the long game: "Just by lengthening the time horizon, you can engage in endeavors that you could never otherwise pursue. At Amazon, we like things to work in five to seven years. We're willing to plant seeds, let them grow—and we're very stubborn. We say we're stubborn on vision and flexible on details."[52]

Change doesn't happen overnight. Rather, as Bezos demonstrates, you must commit time, energy, and resources to finding your true leadership purpose.

The German philosopher Friedrich Nietzsche wrote: "He who has a why to live for, can bear almost any how." The leader's mindset is hardwired for purpose. Without a clearly defined "why" we become less than the sum of our parts. C. R. Snyder, the late psychologist and author of the book *The Psychology of Hope: You Can Get There from Here,* refers to the ability to generate routes to shape the future as "way power" (know direction) and the motivation to move along these routes as "willpower" (determination).[53]

Now look around your own team. Research by Nick Craig and Scott A. Snook, published in the *Harvard Business Review*, found "that fewer than 20% of leaders have a strong sense of their own individual purpose. Even fewer can distill their purpose into a concrete statement."[54] Messages get lost in translation and diluted as they flow up and down and across a company. It doesn't help that leaders often have vastly different and conflicting priorities. Craig and Snook conclude: "It's not what you do, it's how you do your job and why—the strengths and passions you bring to the table no matter where you're seated. Although you may express your purpose in different ways in different contexts, it's what everyone close to you recognizes as uniquely you and would miss most if you were gone."[55]

What is uniquely you? Whatever your answer, you should be clear about it. And if you're not, be ready to find out.

Laszlo Bock, Google's chief people officer, says: "We all want our work to matter. Nothing is a more powerful motivator than to know that you are making a difference in the world."[56] Having a purpose is undeniably helpful for establishing clear direction for the company. Indra Nooyi, chairman and CEO of PepsiCo, one of the world's most iconic and recognized consumer brands, is also the company's chief architect of its "performance with purpose" initiative. On its website Nooyi boldly spells it out in a "letter from the CEO": "Performance with Purpose means just what it says. It is delivering results in the right way, in a sustained way. It means we live our values and do so in a way that fuels our performance. We like to think of it as the way we strive to 'future-proof' PepsiCo."[57]

Your leadership purpose expresses who you are and what you do; it's about leading with intention and making change happen. Amazon's "why" is "to be Earth's most customer centric company; to build a place where people can come to find and discover anything they might want to buy online."[58] When Amazon went public in 1997, its initial public offering (IPO) was anything but conventional. Jeff Bezos wrote a candid letter to shareholders setting out Amazon's vision and why it was going to operate differently than most companies. Bezos puts his why down to three principles: be customer obsessed (not market obsessed); be innovative; and adopt a long-term approach.[59] It is not easy to shape the future, but Bezos's clear-eyed bold action is paying off.

Here are three reasons for finding your why, your leadership purpose.

## Meaning Makers

Human beings are meaning makers. The most ancient part of our brain, the reptilian brain at the back of our head, finds meaning through purpose. In a McKinsey interview with researcher Adam Grant of the University of Pennsylvania's Wharton Business School, Grant explains why purpose matters more than ever: "If you look at the data, what most employees are looking for in their jobs is a sense of meaning and purpose. And when you look at, in turn, what makes work meaningful, what enables people to feel that their daily lives in organizations are significant—more than anything else it's the belief that 'My work makes a difference.' That 'What I do has some kind of benefit or lasting value to other people.' And I think this is something a lot of leaders overlook."[60]

Hans Balmaekers is a leader who understands why a clearly defined leadership purpose matters. He is the CEO and founder of Saam (http://sa.am), a global leadership community with a mission to develop the skills and mindsets for leading change. *Saam* is an African word meaning "together". During our interview, Balmaekers explains: "The name for our organization was born in the break after young leaders expressed they use the word *saam* and a few months later, in October 2014, we were able to welcome our first members onto our leader's platform."

Balmaekers's story began a few years before, when he watched an epic film of the astronaut Ron Garan in space. He says: "It was the beauty of our planet, exposed in a time lapse video shot from the International Space Station (ISS) by astronaut Ron Garan that made me feel absolutely speechless. At the same time, it was his compelling vision that led me to take action: I immediately thought, why not create a community of young leaders across organizations, regions and industries, who'd learn, share and collaborate to solve those big challenges we face as a human race?" Since then, Balmaekers has hosted courses given by inspiring leaders and experts in the fields of sustainability, leadership, and innovation, all with the goal of helping them make a difference and lead the change within their companies.

Balmaekers elaborates: "Especially in the beginning, when it was just an idea, I thought it would be hard to get those experienced and sought-after leaders to contribute an hour of their time to interact with our audience. But simply by sharing the vision, showing my passion and determination, the response was breathtaking."

## Cut Through the Noise

Purpose is an essential strategic tool for cutting through distractions and engaging those around you to get the job done. Remember, when you say yes to something you say no to something else. It's easier to waste time when you don't know what your purpose is. The social media site Facebook knows its purpose, and it clearly defines it as giving "people the power to share and make the world more open and connected."[61] That big, long-term goal helps Facebook founder Mark Zuckerberg filter through the barrage of distractions and guide every big decision he makes. This in turn helps Facebook sustain itself during tough times and overcome challenges by remembering its true purpose. Speaking at a D8 Conference in 2010, Zuckerberg said: "I've always focused on a couple of things. One is [to] have a clear direction for the company and what we build. And the other is just trying to build the best team possible toward that… I think, as a company—having a clear direction on what you are trying to do, and bringing in great people who can execute stuff—then you can do pretty well."[62]

### Best Personal Self

Your "best possible self" (BPS) is the overlap between purpose (your reason for being), talent (your skills and strengths), and effort (your determination). It's the sweet spot, or as English author Sir Kenneth Robinson describes it, "your element." Your BPS is a hidden driver of high performance for you and your team. In the *Journal of Positive Psychology*, researchers Peters, Flink, Boersma, and Linton showed that leaders who imagine a "best possible self" for one minute and then immediately wrote down their thoughts generated a significant increase in positive outlook. The researchers concluded that imagining a positive future could indeed increase expectations for a positive future.[63]

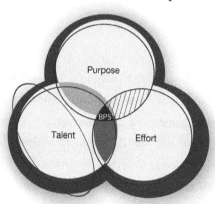

*Unlock Your Best Possible Self*

To unlock your BPS, you must be eager to embark on a journey of self-discovery, learning, and renewal. Ancient Greek thinking summed it up best in two words, inscribed on the forecourt of the temple of Apollo at Delphi: *gnothi seauton*— "Know thyself."

## THE PURPOSE GENERATION

The Millennial generation is more purposeful than any other in history. They care about the "why". In July 2013, twenty-eight-year-old Karen

X. Cheng became a YouTube sensation when she released a video diary of how she learned to dance like a pro in just 365 days. Each and every day she would practice with herculean levels of discipline. Nothing stood in her way. Flu, tiredness, and occasional days when she simply did not want to dance were pushed aside in the pursuit of her goal. This social experiment quickly went viral around the world, gaining over four million views within days. Cheng writes in *Fast Company*: "When you find something you're truly passionate about, it will prioritize itself. You've heard the advice before: do what you love."[64] The lesson here: to make your own mark, you must first match purpose with talent and effort, then a chemical reaction will start that will enable rapid growth beyond anything you thought possible. (To watch Cheng in action, visit www.youtube.com/karenxcheng.)

Business literature now emphasizes how Millennials are more positive and will stay around longer if there is a why they can believe in even if they are unhappy with their paycheck. Deloitte, in its seminal 2014 Millennial Survey, reports that "75 percent of the global workforce by 2025 want to work for organizations that foster innovative thinking, develop their skills, and wish to see them make a positive contribution to society. The study also reveals that Millennials believe companies are not currently doing as much as they could to develop their leadership skills and that they need to nurture their future leaders, especially as they cannot count on them biding their time until senior positions arise."[65] Purpose is at the core of why Millennials get up in the morning.

## LEADERSHIP CANVAS

There are three leaders in all of us: the leader we think we are, the leader others think we are, and the leader we really are. Whether you are leading others or leading yourself, you must accept that your normal mindset simply won't get you to where you want to be. You must find your best mindset more and do so every day. In a *Fast Company* interview, Apple CEO Tim Cook says: "Steve [Jobs] felt that most people live in a small box. They think they can't influence or change a lot of things. I think he would probably call that a limited life."[66] What boxes are you limiting yourself to? Many leaders are drifting, at best not listening, not supporting, and not leading either themselves or others.

In his bestselling book *Behind the Cloud: The Untold Story of How Salesforce.com Went from Idea to Billion-Dollar Company—and Revolutionized an Industry*, CEO Marc Benioff reveals what he learned from Oracle legend Larry Ellison. He writes: "Always have a vision. Be passionate. Act confident, even when you're not."[67] Done well, this is a catalyst for action.

Do you put leadership purpose and vision at the heart of your everyday actions?

### Leadership Purpose
- Why do you do what you do?
- Complete the sentence: My leadership purpose is _____.
- Do you live it daily?
- Imagine five years ahead and describe your ultimate vision for yourself and your organization.
- How often do you get to do what you do best every day?
- How do you put your leadership purpose to work more?

### Values
- What is vital to you?
- What makes someone a real hero?
- What makes you happy?
- Which leaders do you admire and why?
- What principles do you choose to lead by?
- When you fall or have a setback, how do you pick yourself up?

**Vision**

- What do you like most about the vision?
- Describe the vision in one sentence.
- How can you support the vision?
- How well are you performing against the vision?

**Culture**

- Describe your culture in one word.
- What kind of people are you hiring?
- What talent do you attract?
- What makes someone a role model?
- Which companies do you admire and why?
- What do you like most about your culture?
- How will I sustain all of the above?

## CHIEF ENTREPRENEUR OFFICER

Nick Woodman is the founder of global success story GoPro, the video and camera company. Born on June 24, 1975, he grew up in Menlo Park, California, and earned a bachelor's degree in Visual Arts from the University of California, San Diego. His story offers a fascinating lesson about putting purpose at the heart of everything you do. He says: "I feel like in a world where we all try to figure out our place and our purpose here, your passions are one of your most obvious guides."[68]

You can trace Woodman's incredible trajectory of success all the way back to his first passion, surfing. Those who thrive know that if you do what you love you'll be happier and probably perform at a higher level. This chimes with one of entrepreneur Richard Branson's best maxims: "When an opportunity involves adventure, you can be sure I will say yes, yes, yes."[69] This mindset of unapologetic self-discovery led Woodman to choose the University of California, San Diego, where he could merge his love of surfing with a degree in visual arts.

During this time, Woodman took up photography and, without knowing it, had turned on the creative engines of what would become GoPro. It takes nerve to ignore what others expect you to be and listen to your own inner voice. Stepping into new worlds and exploring the unfamiliar helps leaders form bridges to worlds they don't walk within yet. This is a proven strategy for sourcing new ideas and exploring unmet dreams. On GoPro's website, Woodman states: "We dream— we all have passionate ideas about what is possible in life. This passion leads us to pursue experiences that expand our world and inspire those around us."[70]

Yet sometimes we get trapped in boxes too early in life and sacrifice our life's purpose as a result. The voice of reason can be our own worst enemy: if you overthink, you can guarantee that more headaches will emerge and there will be more reasons not to pursue your goals.

After graduating from the University of California in 1997, Woodman found himself in a place that all leaders have experienced: he felt lost, unsure about what his life's next chapter should be. Still only twenty-two, Woodman did know one thing: he was not going to allow himself to get trapped in the box—the idea of working for someone else filled him with abject fear, and he was determined not to do it. He liked building things and dreamed of being a successful entrepreneur. He decided to give himself until age thirty to make it, knowing that it would take huge amounts of sweat and tears and long hours to turn his idea into reality. Woodman had inadvertently begun a journey that would transform his destiny.

His first venture was Fun Bug, a social gaming site that ultimately ended in failure. It ran out of money—$4 million—in just two years. It's likely Woodman's idea would have been a massive hit today, but its doom was sealed when it was launched at the height of the dotcom bubble in 2000. Woodman was humbled by his failure, but he learned some invaluable lessons. First, he had proven to himself that he had the instincts to succeed; second, he had smashed through many comfort zones to secure $4 million in funding. Woodman had learned the importance of never wasting a good mistake, and, as he said in an interview with the British newspaper *The Telegraph*: "It helps if you're working on something that you are immensely passionate about. And when I look at where I succeeded as an entrepreneur and failed as an entrepreneur, I succeeded in the areas I was passionate, and I failed in the areas I wasn't."[71]

At just twenty-six, Woodman held on strongly to the belief that he could still realize his dream. With some small savings, he decided to reconnect with his twin passions of surfing and photography and go on a five-month trip around Australia and Indonesia. He was not a prisoner of his previous failure, and was smart enough to move on. "When I have a difficult decision to make, I imagine myself as a 90-year-old guy looking back on his life. I imagine what I'll think about myself at that point in time, and it always makes it really easy to go for it. You're only going to regret that you've wimped out."[72]

Woodman was excited to get back on the road, where he could find inspiration, clear his head, and meet new people. He still had four years left before he would throw in the towel and get a normal job if he did not meet his goal. Little did he realize that this passion was about to inspire an idea that would later become a flourishing multibillion-dollar company.

Usually, we find inspiration on our travels and then look forward to putting them to work when we return. For Woodman, it was the opposite. He had dreamed up the idea before even arriving in Australia and Indonesia. His trip was a bootstrapping exercise to invent a waterproof wrist camera that could take high-quality close-up action photos of surfers. He solved the problem with a basic 35mm wrist camera attached to the palm of his hand with rubber bands and lots of experimentation. He says: "When you're pursuing your passions, you're turned on. You're with your friends. Some of our best products were born out on the surf or on the mountain or in the air, not in a boardroom."[73]

Woodman became his very own human research and development (R&D) experiment, improvising, bootstrapping, and even selling shell necklaces from his camper van in order to survive. He tested his wrist camera idea in Bali, Indonesia, and knew he had turned his passion into a new invention. He cut his trip short to return home and start what would become GoPro. Woodman felt he'd let down the backers of his first enterprise, Fun Bug, and needed to prove he could be a success. He worked day and night pushing himself to the limit to get GoPro off the ground.

A leader's mindset must embrace the creative edge. It requires sustained effort and mental strength, but the rewards are worth it. Multiply that mindset by ten for your whole team and you have

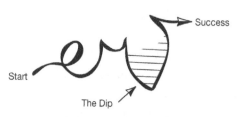

*Success Is Never Linear*

mobilization—a loyal group of followers. Woodman's first company had been a failure, forcing him to dig deep to start all over again, and yet he used the fear of failure and the idea of working for someone else to drive him forward. Success is never linear. It looks more like a squiggle with the biggest dip happening just before you make it.

In 2002, the twenty-six-year-old Woodman finally launched GoPro with just $64,000 of his own startup capital, followed by more funding by close family and friends. He had a clear and singular vision to build versatile high-quality cameras for people who wanted to capture passionate moments and new perspectives. Felix Baumgartner, the Red Bull parachutist, promoted the magic of wearable camera technology when he used multiple GoPro cameras to capture his record-breaking jump to earth in 2014.

Today, according to *Forbes* magazine, Woodman has a net worth of $2.5 billion and leads over 1,000 employees at his company's San Mateo, California headquarters.[74] GoPro is now a household name, doubling in sales every year, and is even used in Hollywood productions for smash hits such as *Homeland*.

From Woodman's story, there are five takeaway messages to remember.

### Do Faster than Doubt

If you want to do something, you must "do faster than doubt". Like a boxing match, in the ring on the left corner we have "do"—that's the belief that tomorrow can be better than today. In the right corner of the ring, we have the opponent, "doubt"—that's the fear that you will fail. The faster you act, the more certain you will become, getting quick wins and building up momentum. Wait too long and doubt will grow until it becomes a titanium wall of resistance. You no longer have the mental toughness, the "willpower" and "way power" to get up.

All this can happen in the blink of an eye. Woodman showed that hope is not a strategy and that you must ring-fence what's essential and then draw the battle lines and get to work.

### FAIL (From Action I Learn)

Woodman had to face every type of fear and experience his fair share of personal disappointments. He's taken failure from taboo to the table, recovering quickly from setbacks and showing that it is possible to turn a passion into a business. In Silicon Valley, it's normal to ask, "So how many times have you failed?" and "Which ones hurt most?" One venture capitalist I know will only back entrepreneurs who have failed big at least three times. Optimism matters too: focusing more on possibility rather than problems is mandatory. Speaking at a Disrupt conference in 2013, Woodman said: "Luck is about being prepared for when the opportunity presents itself."[75]

When you take a risk, such as starting your own company or taking over a new team, challenges will occur as sure as night follows day. Leadership is a decision: you choose to learn from the challenges or let them defeat you. The Latin root meaning of the word "decides" means to cut off, move on, and to let go. The best leaders know when to fight and when to let go. Woodman decided to use failure as a platform from which to think big and launch his idea. You can do that, too.

### The Biggest Risk You Can Take Is Not Taking a Risk

Woodman showed that you must disrupt your usual ways of thinking in order to get started. He gave himself a ten-year timeline to become a top leader and an accomplished entrepreneur. Setting a self-imposed deadline is a proven way to get momentum and close the gap from talk to action. Such constraints require leaders to rediscover their essential purpose and improvise new ways of doing things. In this case, it was Woodman bootstrapping his idea on a shoestring using basic materials such as rubber bands and cellophane tape.

### Connect the Dots

Woodman connects the dots for everyone at GoPro. That means big-picture talk (shaping the future) and detail talk (making it happen). He paints a vivid picture of the future using storytelling and purpose-oriented words such as "we", "our", and "us" that help the team feel what the late author and physician Oliver Sacks called the "the three Bs: bonding, belonging and believing." Passion is imperative, too. Woodman says: "If I didn't follow my passion for surfing… I would have never come up with the concept to make a wrist camera."[76]

Strive to help everyone feel part of the purpose and live by it daily. The personal touch matters so widen the circle of involvement and ask others what the vision personally means to them and how they can support it. A big obstacle today is how to create an environment where everybody brings their best selves to work. The manager era is over. Individuals expect more autonomy and involvement in all aspects of their roles. If they don't like it, they vote with their feet. That's why purpose has such a transformative effect. Make sure individuals embrace the organization's purpose and take pride in their personal contributions to it. It's the best way not just to attract talent but to keep it.

## Lead Change

Woodman pushed the team to keep reinventing and adapting to survive. One of your most urgent roles is to create a shared mindset for the organization and to remove mental or emotional barriers to change. A useful formula for creating a mindset advantage for the company is:

$$(\text{Shared Mindset} + \text{Alignment}) \times \text{Execution at speed}$$

Take care to mobilize everyone in the company to own the vision. Now you have a movement. Have alignment talks to keep everyone focused on executing top priorities quickly. This means delegating, clarifying, allocating resources, and, most importantly, celebrating individual and team success.

Be ready to innovate all your internal processes including your annual performance review. Many forward-thinking companies, such as Accenture, Deloitte, and Adobe Systems, have already eschewed this much over-hyped process in favor of more frequent real-time feedback based on individual assignments. Allocating so much effort and resources on a once-a-year process runs the risk of it simply becoming a bureaucratic tick box exercise or worse, delaying vital performance-related conversations that should happen daily.

As a leader, you have to mesh an individual's sense of purpose with that of the organization. Doug Conant, former CEO of Campbell Soup, writes in a *Harvard Business Review* article, "Your employees are not mind-readers."[77] Make sure you declare what really matters and why and then ensure you deliver on those expectations. At Pixar, the animation company, leaders adopt daily reviews or "dailies", a process for giving and getting immediate feedback in a positive way. Individuals want to know how they're doing. One of the most useful actions you can take today is to give your team regular progress updates. Frequency really does matter. A once-a-year review in an age where most look at their cell phone more than fifty times a day no longer works.

## SUMMARY

The think big mindset (Future Shaper) boils down to three things: finding your purpose, scaling rapidly, and leading by the principle that the best way to know is to do. Sometimes, your leadership purpose will need to be renewed or even replaced, and that's OK. There will be times when you run off course or even lose your way, like a ship in the fog. Don't become a prisoner to a purpose that no longer serves you or, worse, is hurting you or holding you back. Knowing when to let go is as crucial as finding your purpose in the first place. We often give up the search far too quickly and are left with the painful regret of never realizing our full potential.

Even as an adult it is possible to have a brilliant "second act". In chapter three, you'll unlock the next essential mindset to win in the age of disruption—how to act bold (Risk Taker).

## CHAPTER 3

# ACT BOLD MINDSET (RISK TAKER)

*"Innovation distinguishes between a leader and a follower."*
— **Steve Jobs**, late co-founder of Apple

**To "Act Bold" (Risk Taker):**

1. Use an action mindset known as *sisu*.
2. Take risks and overcome obstacles.
3. Embrace failure as one-half of success.
4. Stay big by acting small.
5. Be resilient and brave.

## MIKITANI'S PRINCIPLES

Throughout history we tend to remember bold leaders. Try changing the world while being un-bold. Hiroshi Mikitani, known to friends as "Mickey", acts boldly, an alchemy of risk taking and creativity plus the secret sauce: action-oriented optimism. This talented entrepreneur from Japan is the founder and CEO of Rakuten Inc., Japan's answer to Amazon and the seventh most innovative organization, according to Forbes.[78] *Rakuten* means optimism, which is an apt description for a leader on a mission to empower people and society through the Internet. Mikitani is undaunted by the need to innovate.

His first bold action was to introduce a global mindset at the company by requiring all employees to speak English, even in Japan.[79] And in 2014, this self-made billionaire paid $900 million for Viber, the social messaging app just a few days before Facebook acquired WhatsApp.[80]

Courage and a spirit of adventure are pivotal to Mikitani's mindset. "If we are to be a company that constantly improves, we must have a spirit of experimentation. It does not mean all ideas will be perfect either. They won't. If this happens, we have not failed. We can be secure in our knowledge that we fully explored the possibility."[81]

Mikitani was born in Kobe, Japan, in March 1965, and attended the prestigious Hitotsubashi University in Tokyo. After graduating in 1988, he joined IBJ (Industrial Bank of Japan), one of the country's most famous banks, and was transferred to the United States, where he completed an MBA at Harvard Business School. From an early age, he started to develop a global outlook, which was to hold him in good stead later in life.

In 1995, tragedy struck when one of Japan's biggest earthquakes hit his hometown. Sadly, Mikitani lost close family members, including an uncle.

The Kobe earthquake was a life-changing experience. Mikitani wondered whether another earthquake would hit some day, taking his own hopes and dreams away. His mind was made up. He was not going to live a life of indecision and regret. Without any concrete plans and against everyone's advice, he decided to leave the comfortable, well-paid world of investment banking to walk into the unknown. In *Marketplace*

*3.0: Rewriting the Rules of Borderless Business,* he shares his journey: "At the age of 31, I did the unthinkable. I quit my job at the Industrial Bank of Japan. To say this broke a rule of traditional Japanese corporate behavior would be an understatement."[82]

The leader's mindset had taken hold. Mikitani's instincts had told him that the Internet was going to change the world and rewrite the rules on everything. He had an idea. Inspired by the ancient marketplaces of Japan, he set up the country's first online marketplace for retailers—no easy feat in a proud but traditional and risk-averse Japan, a country about the same size as California.

Undeterred by the critics and scaremongers, Mikitani went to work with gusto. It's never too late to adopt a bold mindset if you have a good idea and the will to make it happen. Using his own capital of just $200,000 and against all the odds, Rakuten was born.[83] Growth was spectacular as Rakuten caught the world's first Internet bubble and went public in 2000 with an initial market cap of more than $3.7 billion. The timing seemed perfect, but it wasn't long before everything began to unravel, culminating in the devastating dotcom crash of 2001. This caused the market cap of Rakuten to fall off a cliff, dropping to just $5 million.[84]

The dotcom crash of 2001 was a galvanizing experience for Mikitani. It tested his levels of resolve to the limit. Like all successful leaders, he did not give up easily but rather used what seemed like insurmountable obstacles to push forward. Such leaders exude conviction and are driven forward to shatter self-imposed limits. Today, Rakuten Inc. has revenues of more than $5 billion, has more than 12,000 staff members, and is one of Japan's most successful entrepreneurial companies. Mikitani is a leader who believes that anything worth doing is difficult. He enjoys tackling challenges and continues to break down barriers for the next generation of leaders. In examining Mikitani's leadership at Rakuten, there are five winning principles to consider.

### Always Improve, Always Advance

This uses the concept of *kaizen* (continuous improvement), first brought to the world by car giant Toyota.[85] The goal for Mikitani is not to change in one day. "I once heard this story: a man in search of wisdom opened a book from a sword-fighting school of the Edo period (1603–1868). Inside, there was just one phrase: 'Myself of today will triumph over myself of yesterday.' This is a beautifully distilled version of *kaizen*. The goal is not to be great overnight, but to be better each day, knowing that this accumulation of improvements is the path to success."[86] At Rakuten, this principle is applied to talent—the idea that anyone can improve with the right training, support, and focus. Most people are not working at full capacity and have wildly untapped skills and potential.

In a LinkedIn post, Mikitani spells out his approach to continuous improvement: "[A]nd now here is the secret: you can look at this from a mathematical point of view. Calculate 1.01 to the 365th power. Even if you could only achieve 1 percent improvement each day—1 percent kaizen per day—at the end of one year, your result is thirty-seven times better than when you started. Try it. You have nothing to lose and a 37x improvement to gain."[87]

Asking a leader or a team to become great overnight is probably unrealistic. But if you adopt a leader's mindset of continuous iteration over time, imagine what could be achieved in 365 days!

### Be Passionately Professional

For Mikitani, being passionately professional means being emotionally and psychologically committed to the job. Like the Adidas poster that celebrates with the motto "All In", it's about everyone taking pride in their own leadership. Leaders who are passionate (they use their heart) and professional (they use their brains) act like catalysts within an organization; they raise the tempo, energy, and therefore the results. At a biochemical level, anyone with the leader's mindset appreciates that even a mood can raise or destroy the morale of a team.

The bad news is that many people's commitment at work has been declining. Gallup's yearly study, "The State of the American Manager: Analytics and Advice for Leaders", concludes: "Of the approximately 100 million people in America who hold full-time jobs, 30 million (30%) are engaged and inspired at work, so we can assume they have a great boss. At the other end of the spectrum are roughly 20 million (20%) employees who are actively disengaged. These employees, who have bosses from hell that make them miserable, roam the halls spreading discontent. The other 50 million (50%) American workers are not engaged. They're just kind of present, but not inspired by their work or their managers."[88] Are you and your team passionately professional? Do you do the basics brilliantly every day? These are must-have considerations in order to build and sustain a fully engaged organization.

### Hypothesize—Practice—Validate—*Shikumika*

*Shikumika* is the Japanese word for "systemize". Mikitani expands: "In this principle, I ask Rakuten employees to ensure that the best ideas rise to the top. When you look at the first two principles—*kaizen* and passionately professional—you can see two ways that I have encouraged employees to strive for greatness and go above and beyond the parameters of their daily assignments. Given those instructions, it's helpful to have a clear framework for all that passion and improvement so that it does not create chaos. This framework comes from the concept and practice of *shikumika*."[89]

Principle 3 is about creating a culture of experimentation. This requires the analytical skills of the hedgehog and the open, curiosity-driven qualities of the fox. How easy is it to generate ideas and test new concepts? Consider what your framework is for idea generation and build an expectation among your peers that they'll receive extra credit at work for debunking old, outdated ways of thinking.

## Maximize Customer Service

This means resources to cope with demand and exceeding expectations by 10X at every turn. Zappos, the online retailer, aims to deliver "happiness" to the customer, while Amazon has achieved global success from its "one click" ordering service. Mikitani writes: "When I talk about maximizing customer satisfaction, I am not thinking about only the end user—for instance, the woman who will buy rice from a Rakuten merchant. I look instead at all the customers who exist in my ecosystem. That rice merchant is also my customer. Should I not also want to maximize his satisfaction?"[90] What happens on the inside of the organization will inevitably be mirrored on the outside. To succeed at maximizing customer service, you must be the leader who you would want to follow.

## Speed! Speed! Speed!

The biggest principle at Rakuten is speed. Mikitani concludes: "As a company grows, there are many roadblocks to speed. Often, workers value caution, and that works against speed. Everyone wants to hang back and see how the leadership will go, allowing them to follow rather than lead. To counter this, I've made it clear that I desire speed, not perfection. I would rather make quick forward progress and then fix what is wrong along the way than hold back until all possible fixes have been made. Waiting for perfection is not an option. Without speed, a company cannot lead."[91]

Fast-growing companies use speed capital in tandem with financial and human capital. They understand that they are now operating in a high-velocity world where the leaders' job is to inspire everyone to deliver more. To do that, you need to develop the next generation of talent that is committed to learning and growth.

## THINK LIKE A STARTUP

Silicon Valley is 1,500 square miles of the most fertile ground on the planet and a giant launch pad for some of the world's most well-known startups. Cisco Systems, Intel, eBay, and Hewlett-Packard are just some of the companies that have made it their home. What makes this area unique is a combination of access to capital, talent, and innovation. In the Bay area alone, more than 90 percent of companies have an innovation strategy supported by their top team. What's telling is, irrespective of size, they cultivate a belief system that with the right mindset anything is possible. Success is no longer about being big or small. It's about speed and rapid scaling such as the technology firm Slack Technologies, Inc., or coffee pioneer Starbucks.

In our lifetime, technology has advanced at an extraordinary rate (the first web browser was only invented in 1994 and the first iPhone in 2007). Research by Boston Consulting Group illustrates the time it's taken for each one of the following inventions to reach 100 million users:[92]

- Telephone: 75 years
- Web: 7 years
- Facebook: 4 years
- Instagram: 2 years

Ernst and Young (EY), the global professional services firm, puts a startup mindset at the heart of its culture. EY asked more than 1,000 individuals working in big companies how they felt about work today. Only three out of ten respondents agreed their organization had a startup mindset.[93]

Every big company can stay big by acting small. The three biggest obstacles leaders must overcome in order to unlock a startup mindset are:

1.  **Organizational barriers.** Status quo mindset, bureaucracy, and fear are some of the biggest innovation killers. Fear is the enemy of innovation: fear of judgment, fear of the unknown, and fear of losing your job can prevent the best-intentioned leader or team from changing. To encourage innovation, a leader must incentivize risk taking and put creativity at the heart of its culture. Leaders own the culture and must model the behaviors they want to see their teams display.

2.  **Cognitive barriers.** The demands on leaders' time make it hard for the brain to think clearly. Thanks to unhealthy eating and sleeping habits, our brains are rarely in peak condition. Information overload, old habits, and sloppy thinking can literally stop innovation in its tracks. I worked with one forward-thinking organization that held "walk and talk" meetings and met in different locations every week to stay upbeat. The best leaders let their minds wander. Take a brain break: go for a walk and get some fresh air. This is often where great ideas lie dormant.

3.  **Schlep blindness:** Paul Graham, cofounder of Y Combinator, is credited with this useful expression. He explains: "There are great startup ideas lying around unexploited right under our noses. One reason we don't see them is a phenomenon I call *schlep blindness. Schlep* was originally a Yiddish word but has passed into general use in the US. It means a tedious, unpleasant task."[94] Leaders are often guilty of schlep blindness, adopting avoidance behaviors such as procrastination or making excuses, which ensures that a potential idea dies early. The best strategy

is to just dive right in. Don't wait. Don't overthink, and when you hit a wall, take a break or move into a new environment. To overcome schlep blindness, write your fears down and bounce ideas around with the team. Ideas usually go through a series of stages from "that's a bad idea" to "that's a good idea" and then finally "that's my idea". Graham says ideas can be obvious but hard, easy, and overcrowded, or not obvious but hard.[95] Be open to hidden insights: prototype ideas quickly until they make sense and remember most good ideas start as bad ideas.

If leaders follow the well-trodden path and refuse to embrace disruption, their very existence becomes threatened. Who would have predicted that the technology company Kodak would file for Chapter 11 bankruptcy, car manufacturer Volkswagen would find itself at the center of a public relations disaster and that the once mighty smartphone manufacturer Blackberry would lose its way?

In a knowledge economy, it's about managing rapid evolution where business models are upended and change is the norm. Startups have huge advantages in this new world. They adapt quickly, duck hazards, and grab opportunities faster than their larger, sleepier competitors. They must also work within tight constraints that can force more creativity. And they're often expected to own their work and challenge established ways of doing things. *Forbes* magazine columnist Josh Linkner writes: "While big companies are busy protecting the golden goose with fear-based, micro improvements, startups are busy changing the world."[96]

## STAYING BIG BY ACTING SMALL

Zappos is no stranger to staying big by acting small. One of its core values is "to embrace and drive change." Headed up by CEO Tony Hsieh, it has won credit around the world for its 3-Day Culture Camp and School of WOW. On the Zappos blog, one employee writes: "One of the many things that Zappos has done to make my list of favorite things is that this company never stops surprising me. Big surprises, little surprises, all kind of surprises. The biggest reason I love Zappos is because they let me be me, the real me. I have never felt more comfortable in my own skin than I have since day one here."[97] Let those words sink in. Do they hold true for you and your company culture?

In 2015, Zappos made the controversial decision to completely rethink how its company operates by implementing a new way of working called "holacracy". This system, described in Frederic Laloux's book *Reinventing Organizations: A Guide to Creating Organizations Inspired by the Next Stage of Human Consciousness,* removes traditional hierarchies such as job titles, manager roles, departments, and organizational charts. It's like a giant silo buster on steroids. Teams self-organize to get the most urgent work done, and individuals are more empowered to behave like an owner of the company. Individual contributors have the freedom to challenge established thinking and are incentivized to find faster, better ways of doing things. Every leader can benefit from this.

## INNOVATION IN A BOX

Adobe, the computer software company headquartered in California, is like one giant startup in which everyone is encouraged to think innovatively, irrespective of job title. You've probably tried one of Adobe's popular software products, such as Adobe Reader or Adobe Photoshop. Founded in 1985, the company has more than 13,500 employees and has continued to reinvent itself to stay at the forefront of technology changes. Companies wax lyrical about the need to be more innovative but rarely make it part of their culture. It's a bit like telling someone to smile and be happy when they're not. And let's face it; most offices are the worst environments to be innovative. When you have to step out of the office to be creative, you know there's a problem. Low ceilings, poor lighting, endless meetings, and a lack of fresh air render the brain incapable of a single creative spark.

Adobe is different. Mark Randall, Adobe's vice president of creativity, is a champion of acting boldly. Speaking at the 2014 Lean Startup Conference, he tells the story of how Adobe found a new way of innovating. Like most companies, Adobe has transitioned from being a product company to delivering software via cloud technology. In the past, Adobe tested, evaluated, and sought feedback from customers on up to a dozen products every year. "We might spend from $100 up to $1 million on each one of those projects," says Randall. [98]

Now the focus is on creating a culture of innovation. A new approach, known as Adobe Kickbox, enables it to do several hundred projects for less money than it had cost to do a dozen previously. How has this been possible? Randall explains: "Innovation is a long-term investment and we want to build innovators, not just innovations. So the key has been equipping our people with the skills and the experience they need to innovate and that means experiencing not only succeeding as an innovator but experiencing failing as an innovator." [99]

Adobe Kickbox is best described as "innovation in a box". A red box contains everything an Adobe employee needs to turn an idea into reality, including a $1,000 prepaid credit card, instructions, and even a Starbucks coffee gift and candy! (Since the fifteenth century, coffee has been touted as the answer for waking up your mind.) The excitement doesn't end with the red box. Once the employee has completed it, he or she is presented with a blue box. What's in it remains a mystery. What's for certain is that Adobe not only thinks like a startup but also acts like one, and along the way it has made its employees fall in love with the company all over again.

## THE BRAIN TRUST

A great leader builds a work culture where people can debate ideas, alert others to concerns, and criticize openly. But as any organization grows, openness and candor are sometimes the first casualties. It becomes easier to leave things unsaid, and typically there is a failure to act until a situation has reached the crisis point. It's not uncommon for managers to filter bad news to protect the CEO from bad news.

On the flip side, the best work cultures help people to "tell it how it is" without fear of recrimination. Ed Catmull's killer app, the Pixar Brain Trust, helps build a candid culture. Catmull is the CEO of Pixar, the animation giant responsible for groundbreaking films such as *The Incredibles*, *Monsters Inc.*, and *Toy Story*. In the *Harvard Business Review*, Catmull outlined his key leadership principles:[100]

1.  Everyone must have the freedom to communicate with anyone.
2.  It must be safe for everyone to offer ideas.
3.  We must stay close to innovations happening in the academic community.

The Brain Trust is made up of the top team, a small group of leaders who oversee the development of Pixar's animated films. Its purpose is to put hierarchy to the side and focus on straight talk about the ideas and direction of a movie. It's not a brainstorming meeting per se. Rather, it's run as a board of mentors whose role is to be completely open, honest, and direct about content and ideas. They offer support but, crucially, no one has the authority to tell the production team what to do. At the end of a meeting, they must decide what to use and what to ignore.

Says Catmull: "When a director and producer feel in need of assistance, they convene the group (and anyone else they think would be valuable) and show the current version of the work in progress. This is followed by a lively two-hour give-and-take discussion, which is all about making the movie better. There's no ego. Nobody pulls any punches to be polite. This works because all the participants have come to trust and respect one another. They know it's far better to learn about problems from colleagues when there's still time to fix them than from the audience after it's too late. The problem-solving powers of this group are immense and inspirational to watch."[101]

A Brain Trust is different than a standard meeting. It brings together a group of leaders who are explicitly asked to be candid, to speak the truth on a daily basis. The net effect is individuals taking more pride in their work and more responsibility for their decisions. Now *that's* a winning culture.

## THE *SISU* LAB

Like modern-day explorers ascending K2 or reaching the North Pole, a leader's mindset has what the Finnish call *sisu*, a flair for "extraordinary determination and resoluteness in the face of extreme adversity". It takes *sisu* to stand at the door when a big angry bear is on the other side. That bear could be your competition or even a deep-seated inner fear holding you back from a better future.

Emilia Lahti (www.emilialahti.com) heads up the Sisu Lab and is a distinguished researcher of the Finnish construct of *sisu*. She holds an applied positive psychology Masters degree from the University of Pennsylvania and has been mentored in the fields of grit, self-control, and positive psychology by world-renowned thought leaders Dr. Martin Seligman and Dr. Angela Duckworth.

Lahti is the embodiment of *sisu*. Her work stems from a traumatic experience that made her rethink her whole life and ultimately find her true calling: helping others. In the long term, she wants to identify practical ways for the cultivation of *sisu* within various contexts, from being a leader to recovering from traumatic experiences. She writes: "Evolution comes before survival only in the dictionary. We are creatures of reason, programmed to preserve energy and maintain equilibrium. However, in order to not merely survive but to thrive, we must occasionally crank our comfort-o-meter to the red zone. Having an 'action mindset' will help you bear the initial discomfort and reap the ultimate rewards."[102]

You can watch her captivating talk about the power of *sisu* at www. ted.com/emilalahti.

In an interview, I spoke with Lahti about *sisu*'s role as a hidden driver of a leader's mindset around the world.

TERENCE MAURI: What is *sisu*?

EMILIA LAHTI: *Sisu* refers to our ability to go beyond our preconceived physical and mental capacities. It is the ability to take extraordinary action and stay determined when all odds are against us. One of its underlying premises is that there is more strength to us than meets the eye. How *sisu* differs from perseverance and grit is that it's more about the short-term intensity than about long-term endurance. It is our ability to take action against impossible odds, transform barriers into frontiers, exceed ourselves, and see beyond the limitations of the present moment. One could define it as the second wind of mental endurance or the sixth gear of tenacity. It's not something you would tap into all the time but a force that allows you to push through the unimaginable.

TM: I think *Harry Potter* author J. K. Rowling is a prominent example of *sisu*. She was rejected more than 130 times before she got noticed. According to legend, one publisher even told her "not to give up the day job." We know what happened after that. The *Harry Potter* series became one of the most successful film franchises ever, grossing more than $6 billion. On receiving an honorary degree from Harvard

University, Rowling gave a heartfelt commencement speech titled "The Fringe Benefits of Failure, and the Importance of Imagination". She told the audience: "Ultimately, we all have to decide for ourselves what constitutes failure. But the world is quite eager to give you a set of criteria if you let it. Failure means a stripping away of the inessential. I stopped pretending to myself to be anything other than what I was, and began to direct all my energy into finishing the only work that mattered to me. Had I really succeeded at anything else, I might never have found the determination to succeed in the one arena where I believe I truly belonged. Rock bottom became the solid foundation on which I built my life."[103]

Rowling is now a successful role model for millions of people around the world. They draw strength from her courage and unflagging determination to not give up.

What is the main benefit of *sisu*?

EL: All of the great advancements of humanity and the progress of modern society are based on our ability to expand our psychological horizon, take a step into the unknown, and make a path where there is none. What this means is that we have to go beyond our comfort zone, try out new skills, and become learners. Whoever is able to tolerate this can become a leader and inspire those around her or him to replicate the same behavior. I argue that having this ability is not a luxury but is a necessity if we are to create a more positive human future. Now more than perhaps ever, we need the ability to imagine a new future and take action. Remaining complacent will stall progress, and it's those with an entrepreneurial mind that can lead the intellectual quest for our humanity.

Entrepreneurship is a mindset and does not refer to only those who set up a startup. I think the challenges of running a startup are often overstated, as it is very rarely that the costs of failure go beyond a slight dent on one's self-esteem. In fact, Silicon Valley has done a great job in re-imagining failure as a badge of honor.

TM:  I agree. Take FailCon founder Cass Phillipps. She helps leaders to learn from their own and others' failures. The company's motto is "Embrace your mistakes. Build your success."[104] Picking yourself up off the ground after yet another setback gets tiring after a while. FailCon aims to turn failure into a process for instant learning and reflection. In Latin, "reflect" means to refold, which suggests we look backward in order to move forward. As the nineteenth-century philosopher Søren Kierkegaard wrote, "Life can only be understood backwards; but it must be lived forward."[105]

At FailCon, in the course of a one-day conference, peers share stories of what went wrong and inspire each other with lessons learned to move forward. While most cultures just talk about success, it helps to organize a friendly peer forum to explore failure. FailCon now has a thriving community of locations where FailCon events are held, including Tokyo, Berlin, and Singapore. How could you adopt the FailCon principles in your company? Apple U, the Apple University, was part of Steve Jobs's legacy to not only help future employees live Apple's values but also to learn from past failures and triumphs in a more systematic way.

How can leaders tap the power of *sisu*?

EL:  We can learn from the research in related fields. I would describe *sisu* as a set of tools or a bundle of strategies that one can use to tap into their inner core strength. Whatever tools work best depends on the individual. There is no one size fits all. Research shows us that for mental strength in extreme adversity, social support, one's ability to remain curious, and the availability of useful mental strategies are crucial. Most of these can be obtained and practiced through conscious effort. One's ability to reflect and pause can ultimately mean the difference between success and failure when the going gets tough. The limits of our thinking mean the limits of our possibilities.

TM: Is *sisu* learnable?

EL: Preliminary studies show that people believe it is. This actually plays a part in the process. Stanford University professor and motivation expert Carol Dweck has found that our beliefs regarding our abilities are the biggest indicator of our future actions.[106] Similarly to resilience, I propose that *sisu* is something that is tied to our experiences, learning, and mindset. I suggest that part of the power of *sisu* lies in its creativity and hope-inducing nature (hope is the sparkplug of all action, as we know from the research of Dr. Shane Lopez, and creativity enables us to imagine potential solutions to a problem). It invokes visions of one's future self. If we dare to see beyond our present situation and capacity, we start to act and move toward our goals, pushing past our barriers. To expose the mind to a story is to prospect and imagine future scenarios and possibilities.

Furthermore, an action mindset contributes to how we approach obstacles. I would describe it as akin to signing up for a marathon or an Ironman before you have any clue what you are actually doing. It provides a daring "leap before you look" attitude, so we are not paralyzed by the idea of what might go wrong.

TM: What final techniques will help leaders cultivate a *sisu* mindset?

EL: One of the first steps is to become aware of one's thought patterns and realize that our behavior is malleable. This will require a lot of work, and I don't believe that shortcuts exist. It is about fostering one's character and the result of all the experiences as well as our genetic dispositions.

It all comes down to awareness of our values and actions and making the decision to reach beyond one's capacities. We don't know what we can do before we push beyond our mental barriers. Try to find ways to grow those around you. For example, how am I encouraging the *sisu* of others? We are all deeply interconnected and have great power to open doors for each other but also close them. Leaders include *everyone* because I believe it all starts with personal leadership, and we must take responsibility.

Ultimately, leaders should aim to empower others and facilitate the "*sisu* mindset" for those around them. The greatest things are born from trust. Courage is of special importance when we face obstacles. Malala Yousafzai is a global symbol of courage and also the youngest ever Nobel Peace Prize laureate in history. Yousafzai is a Pakistani school pupil and education activist who was targeted and shot by extremists on her way to school for defending her right to an education. After a long road to recovery, Malala is back and more determined than ever to keep making her voice heard.

Still a teenager, she is a vocal activist for female education, was featured in *Time* magazine's "The 100 Most Influential People in the World",[107] and speaks at the World Economic Forum and the United Nations, raising awareness of women's rights around the world.

## THE *SISU* LEADER

Dominican entrepreneur Jésus Blanco is a strong advocate of *sisu*. He is the CEO of Linktia (www.linktia.com), a group of market-leading companies specializing in content production, talent management, online platforms, and technology solutions. His story is a blueprint for increasing your *sisu* quotient and overcoming the toughest of battles to survive. When Blanco was seventeen, tragedy struck his family, when his mother was brutally attacked in a local supermarket in Spain, where they lived. It was a big wake-up call. When I interviewed him exclusively for *The Leader's Mindset,* he said: "Time is our most precious gift. It [the attack] changed my life forever." From that day on, Blanco decided to change lives for the better and become an entrepreneur.

Today, and still only in his thirties, Blanco is responsible for defining Linktia's vision and leading the group's long-term objectives and global business strategy. He is one of the first Dominican graduates of the UK's elite Saïd Business School at Oxford and a postgraduate of Harvard Business School. How did Blanco harness *sisu* and transform his fortunes beyond imagination?

I decided to move to London in order to learn English. My first year in London was transformational. I truly realized the meaning of being poor. I couldn't speak English and had only $2,500 to my name. I didn't know anyone and had to share one room with four people. I didn't have money to eat properly for two months and lent a friend the only money I had left. I was hungry, alone, and couldn't find a job with a budget of just $40 a week.

Every morning I'd be the first to arrive at my local Internet café, where I would spend the day sending CVs to potential employers. I literally survived on the soft drink Dr Pepper and a little food every day; the simple things really brought light to my life at this stage in my journey. I'd reached rock bottom. I'd left my family, my friends, and a secure job in Spain to learn English. These are tests, which tell us how much we want something. I knew I had to go through this journey and would survive. I had to draw upon deep reserves of courage—*sisu*. In one month I sent over 1,000 CVs! Going through hunger changed my life forever. I vowed I wanted to help others to avoid this fate.

When I was at rock bottom, something remarkable happened to me. Sitting in a park, some passersby starting to talk to me in Spanish. It's moments like this that you realize you should always have hope and never give up. It turned out that one of the passersby was leaving her job, which I might be suitable for. As my English was still very basic, I created a script for my CV and memorized it all in two days. A miracle happened. I got my first job opposite the famous Bank of England in the City of London on Threadneedle Street. My hunger period was over, but I can say that without that experience, I would not be the person and leader I am today.

It gave me the belief to continue to break through mental and social barriers. I became one of the first Dominicans to be accepted at Oxford's Saïd Business School, and at thirty-six, I completed my MBA at Harvard. I have a personal formula for success: it's based on what obstacles we overcome. It's about a purpose that is bigger than you, not giving up and losing track of the why. The leader's mindset is a tool to change lives for the better.

## CONNECT TO A HIGHER PURPOSE

Most leaders in Blanco's situation would have given up and boarded a plane for home. Where *sisu* flourishes, leaders report higher levels of hope (unshakeable self-belief), optimism (expecting good things to happen), perseverance (commitment to the purpose and not giving up easily), and resilience (ability to adapt to obstacles and recover quickly).

To tap the leader's mindset faster, commit to building up all four of these qualities, and don't give up easily. Obstacles are essential to them: they help them transcend self-imposed limitations—all the boxes that we choose to live in.

A new study published in the *Journal of Personality and Social Psychology* by researcher Janina Marguc at the University of Amsterdam supports this hypothesis that obstacles induce strength:

> Daily life is full of obstacles: a construction site blocking the usual road to work, a colleague's background chatter interfering with one's ability to concentrate, a newborn child hindering parents in completing their daily routines, or a lack of resources standing in the way of realizing an ambitious plan.
>
> How do people cognitively respond to such obstacles? How do the ways in which they perceive and process information from their environment change when an obstacle interferes with what they want to accomplish? In the present research, we aim to shed light on these questions by investigating the impact of obstacles on global versus local processing. We propose that unless people are inclined to disengage prematurely from ongoing activities, obstacles will prompt them to step back and adopt a more global, Gestalt-like processing style that allows them to look at the "big picture" and conceptually integrate seemingly unrelated pieces of information.[108]

It turns out that overcoming obstacles provides an unexpected motivational boost, pushing you to deliver more than is expected. The stakes are higher but so are the rewards. An illustration of this is the story of Drew Houston, CEO of the startup file sharing company Dropbox. He came up with the idea for the company after he forgot his flash drive and could not work on a long bus ride from Boston to New York.[109]

Brian Chesky, cofounder of Airbnb, equally credits obstacles as part of his leadership development. He writes in his personal blog:

> If you want to understand Airbnb, you have to understand our beginnings. Our story started with a problem that those struggling financially know well. In October of 2007, my roommate Joe Gebbia and I were living in a San Francisco apartment, and we couldn't afford rent. That weekend, an international design conference was coming to town, and all of the hotels were sold out. So we had an idea: why not turn our place into a bed and breakfast for the conference? We inflated airbeds and called it the AirBed & Breakfast.[110]

Today, Airbnb stands at the forefront of the sharing economy with more than 20 million people using its service and winning *Inc.* magazine's "Company of the Year" title. If Chesky and his cofounders had given up at the first major obstacle, there would be no Airbnb, as we know it.

## FAILURE PIONEER

One of the most popular books among leaders is the Roman emperor Marcus Aurelius's *Meditations*. This seminal book is based around a single cogent idea: "You have power over your mind—not outside events. Realize this, and you will find strength."[111] Travis Kalanick, CEO of Uber, the ride-hailing company, would probably be the first to apply this mantra to his own life. Kalanick is a "failure pioneer": he was the unluckiest entrepreneur before karma came back in the form of Uber. At a FailCon Conference in 2011, Kalanick opened his speech by saying: "My previous ten years before Uber are a case study in failure." His story is a model for overcoming obstacles, fighting for what you believe in, and not giving up. In 2015, he was named the *Financial Times*'s Person of the Year in the Boldness in Business Awards category.

Kalanick, who was a UCLA computer engineering student, dropped out in 1998 to start Scour, the Internet's first peer-to-peer file-sharing service, predating Napster. Scour took off quickly, attracting millions of users. In Kalanick's final year at UCLA, he secured funding for it from two LA media moguls who wanted to get on the dotcom bandwagon, but the project ran into funding issues and thirty-three of the largest media companies in the world threatened it with a $250 billion copyright infringement lawsuit. At the time, this was equivalent to Sweden's gross domestic product. Kalanick made a valiant strategic move and declared bankruptcy. "A lot of failure starts with naivety but so does a lot of success," he says.[112]

Just one month later, in January 2001, Kalanick's *sisu* spirit kicked in again, and he launched what he aptly calls his "revenge business", Red Swoosh. Using similar peer-to-peer technology, he would take the thirty-three media companies that sued him the first time around and turn them into loyal paying customers. The problem was that the business model was probably five years too early to the market. Living hand to mouth, Kalanick did not pay himself for more than four years—he called this period his "blood, sweat and ramen years." Undaunted, he continued to pursue his vision, getting close but not quite there. He says: "No matter how hard something is, there's always an end point. It always has to end. Whatever it is. It might last one year or 10 years, but it will end."[113]

For Kalanick, this part of his journey ended on a happy note: in 2007, Red Swoosh was acquired by Akamai Technologies for $19 million.[114] Kalanick is used to being the little guy and is galvanized when he's playing David versus Goliath. He uses fear to transcend limitations. "Fear is the disease," he says. "Hustle is the antidote. Whatever it is that you're afraid of, go after it."[115]

Then came the idea that would change his life. Uber was born on a cold, foggy day in Paris in 2008 from Kalanick's frustration in trying to find a cab. His idea was ingenious: push a button, night or day, and get a cheap, efficient taxi ride. Like all startups, Uber began small as a young, scrappy insurgent. It was the new kid on the block fighting many battles, from regulatory lawsuits to protests that go hand in hand with major industry disruption. China has many Uber copycats, and in Seoul, South Korea, an Uber passenger must not be Korean. Kalanick fights for what he believes in and, arguably, is more successful exactly because he has failed more and learned more. He says: "Stand by your principles and be comfortable with confrontation. So few people are, so when the people with the red tape come, it becomes a negotiation."[116]

Like all outstanding leaders, Kalanick works hard for the vision and purpose. His long-term mission is to go to every major city in the world and roll out an efficient, cost-effective transportation system. Flash forward to 2016 and Uber is already valued at $40 billion, operating in more than fifty-five countries and 300 cities.[117] It has only around 2,000 staff members, but manages more than 160,000 contractors who drive every day—that's a ratio of eighty contractors to one full-time staff member. "To be ubered" has even become a catchphrase for disruptive innovation. In an interview in the *Washingtonian*, Kalanick says: "As an entrepreneur, I try to push the limits, pedal to the metal."[118]

This incredible growth requires the best brains in the business to sustain expansion, and it starts with Kalanick. When he wakes up in the morning he has to attend to two lists: (1) solve problems and

(2) invent cool stuff. "I have a list of the hardest, most challenging problems that our company needs to solve and I start at the top and work my way down," he says. "And I have a list of the coolest most fascinating things that we can invent and I start at the top of the list and work my way down."[119]

It's only when you do that that change happens. Failure is a byword for action. Kalanick has a 10X goal—to make travel as ubiquitous as drinking water. He also has a relentless personality and a plucky attitude toward risk taking.

## SUMMARY

To unlock the bold mindset in your everyday role, do the following.

### Build a Strong Mind

To achieve greatness you have to fail greatly. Hollywood producer and director Jerry Zucker says: "Nobody else is paying as much attention to your failures as you are… To everyone else, it's just a blip on the radar screen, so just move on."[120] Most overnight successes take about ten to fifteen years, and the journey is not a linear path but rather a series of ups and downs with a major dip along the way known as the "test". A test could take the form of financial loss or one of your top performers walking out the door. Try building risk and resilience into your daily routine. MIT Media Lab's Joi Ito tells leaders to focus on "Resilience instead of strength, which means you want to yield and allow failure and you bounce back instead of trying to resist failure."[121]

At times, you might privately think you can't go on. You must persist. Arianna Huffington, cofounder of the *Huffington Post*, says it best: "I failed, many times in my life. One failure that I always remember was when 36 publishers rejected my second book. Many years later, I watched *Huff Post* come alive to mixed reviews, including some very negative ones, like the reviewer who called the site 'the equivalent of *Gigli*, *Ishtar*, and *Heaven's Gate* rolled into one.' But my mother used to tell me, 'failure is not the opposite of success, it's a stepping stone to success.'"[122]

## Eat Problems for Breakfast

You are bound to fail occasionally. In failure are life's little secrets: you cannot learn to ride a bike by reading how to ride one. James Dyson produced more than 5,000 failed prototypes before he invented his bestselling Dyson Air Vacuum. Embrace failure as your biggest teacher. It's a vital part of the process of growing as a human being. A real failure is when you make a mistake and don't fix it quickly and start over. The formula for success isn't a mystery. It's a conscious choice to learn from failure. Each wrong choice builds character and strengthens your mindset for the next challenge.

Stephen Rapoport, founder of Pact Coffee, started Failboat by gathering startup founders around a table to discuss their failures and what they had learned. In an interview in the *Sunday Times*, he says: "I'm absolutely convinced you learn an awful lot more when you get things wrong than when you get things right. When you get things right, you don't know whether you've got them completely right. When you get things wrong, you know where the line is."[123]

Rapoport continues: "We have two modes: success and learning. I don't look at learning as a failure, as long as you don't repeat the same mistakes over and over. If you're scared to fail, you will find it hard to make decisions, you will slow down and you won't want to push yourself. In other words, if you're not failing at all, you may not be trying hard enough."[124]

## Embrace Constraints

Constraints encourage leaders and their teams to think on their feet and rediscover their creativity. Phil Hansen's story is a master class in using the power of constraints. His TED talk, "Embrace the Shake", has received more than 1.7 million views to date and continues to inspire leaders around the world. Hansen, a pointillist, developed an unruly shake in his hand that kept him from doing what he loved best—drawing art. Devastated, he lost his way, not knowing what the future held. After much soul searching, he decided to see a neurologist, who told him to "Embrace the shake and transcend it."

In his TED talk, Hansen explains that "Limitations may be the most unlikely of places to harness creativity, but perhaps one of the best ways to get ourselves out of ruts, rethink categories, and challenge accepted norms. And instead of telling each other to seize the day, maybe we can remind ourselves every day to seize the limitation."[125]

A mindset that embraces constraints is an often mostly overlooked concept but hugely important for a leader's mindset. Scarcity can lead to resourcefulness and an improved work ethic, pushing everyone to think more creatively about finding the best solution to a problem. Next time you give your team or yourself a challenge, remember Hansen's message that limitations can force us to think bigger. Don't assume that having to make do with less is a hopeless challenge. You can pick up more wonderful lessons from Hansen in his book *Tattoo a Banana: And Other Ways to Turn Anything and Everything into Art*.

As you've now seen, think big (Future Shaper) and act bold (Risk Taker) are the first two mindsets to 10X in order to unlock the leader's mindset. They're crucial for leading in a world where to be successful is to evolve. The final mindset is to learn fast (Knowledge Seeker), which we'll explore in depth in chapter 4.

# CHAPTER 4
# LEARN FAST MINDSET (KNOWLEDGE SEEKER)

*"Fast learners win."*

— **Eric Schmidt**, Google

**To "Learn Fast" (Knowledge Seeker):**
1. Connect talent to plans and ideas.
2. Use multiple mentors to raise your game.
3. Build social capital.
4. Use the new science of teamwork.
5. Embrace chance encounters.

## FAST EATS SLOW

Mentors, learning, and even chance meetings are telltale attributes of the leader's mindset. Stanford University psychologist Alfred Bandura has shown the impact of chance encounters and luck on people's lives, writing that "some of the most important determinants of life paths often arise through the most trivial of circumstances."[126]

Sean Parker is no stranger to chance encounters. He is the billionaire entrepreneur who co-founded the file-sharing computer service Napster and became a major player in the launch of Facebook. According to legend, Parker was fascinated by the potential of social networking and actively sought out Mark Zuckerberg for a meeting. When the two early twenty-somethings finally met in a popular restaurant in New York, they hit it off immediately. Parker understood the social networking business model and shared the same excitement and vision as Zuckerberg for helping people connect and make friends.

Then a chance meeting a few months later changed everything. Parker literally ran into Zuckerberg on a random suburban street in Palo Alto, and they instantly hit it off again, just like they had in New York.

It wasn't long before Parker was appointed the founding president of the five-month-old startup and quickly became a close friend and mentor to Zuckerberg, even moving into his house with the rest of the team. According to legendary entrepreneur and Facebook investor Peter Thiel, Parker was the first to see potential in the company to be "really big," and that "if Mark ever had any second thoughts, Sean was the one who cut that off."[127]

I've tried to be open to chance meetings. For example, many years ago I decided to do something completely different on Christmas Day. I had become disenchanted with the holiday—for me, it had lost some of its magic. I felt it was time to give back and think about others less fortunate. I talked to different charities and found one I strongly connected with—on Christmas Day, it provided warm shelter and food to the homeless. I happily volunteered and experienced one of the most humbling yet rewarding days of my life... and what happened three months after that experience highlighted the serendipity of networking. As a thank you, charity organizers invited all the volunteers to a reception at 10 Downing Street, the UK prime minister's residence in London. I remember standing outside the famous black door, in awe of walking in the same footsteps as US president John F. Kennedy, British prime minister Winston Churchill, and president of South Africa Nelson Mandela, to name but a few.

Being open to serendipity and chance meetings doesn't guarantee anything in life or business. The best one can say is this: companies must cheat death multiple times, especially in the early years, in order to survive. If you have access to diverse networks and can tap the brains of a community of mentors, miracles can happen, especially if you work hard for them. This is what makes Silicon Valley unique: there is a freedom to connect and a willingness to help one another.

Paul Graham, cofounder of Y Combinator, says: "Having people around you care about what you're doing is an extraordinarily powerful force. Even the most willful people are susceptible to it. About a year after we started Y Combinator, I said something to a partner at a well-known VC firm that gave him the (mistaken) impression I was considering starting another startup. He responded so eagerly that for about half a second I found myself considering doing it."[128]

Connecting to others is a primary skill for any leader. Simon Sinek, author of *Why Leaders Eat Last*, advocated that networks are not just necessary to our survival as a race but are key for innovation. Ideas festivals such as the Inc. 5000, TED, and WEF have become incredibly popular, reporting record numbers of attendees. We all crave human connection in a world where we are increasingly detached from real human contact. Connecting to others can also help leaders cope with uncertainty and constant flux. In *The Half-Life of Facts: Why Everything We Know Has an Expiration Date*, Samuel Arbesman, a Harvard mathematician, writes: "Knowledge is like radioactivity. If you look at a single atom of uranium, whether it's going to decay—breaking down and unleashing its energy—is highly unpredictable. It might decay in the next second, or you might have to sit and stare at it for thousands, or perhaps even millions, of years before it breaks apart… Facts, in the aggregate, have half-lives."[129]

Arbesman concludes: "Facts change in regular and mathematically understandable ways. And only by knowing the pattern of our knowledge's evolution can we be better prepared for its change."[130]

To combat the half-life of knowledge, leaders must look for new ways to generate maximum value from their knowledge pools. By becoming the "node" in their knowledge pool, leaders become a magnet for opportunities and can tap into a vast pool of resources.

9others.com is one such community that knows ideas occur when humans connect and exchange ideas. It was founded in 2011, on the belief that "your success requires the aid of others." A host and nine others will meet for an informal dinner to mingle, discuss challenges, and share experiences. It already has a network of more than 3,500 entrepreneurs in thirty-three cities and is leading the way with a more intelligent approach to networking.

## HYGGE

To get ahead and learn faster, you should build social capital, the trust, empathy, shared norms, and mutual understanding that underpin any successful business relationship, especially between the leader and a team. You can't build social capital overnight; it's earned on a daily basis. For example, companies such as Danish toy maker Lego build social capital through the principle of *hygge*, pronounced "heu-gah". This is the art of building a strong sense of "we"—a communal space for the *hygge* spirit to flourish.

Margaret Hoffman, TED speaker and author of *Beyond Measures*, says: "In any company, you can have a brilliant bunch of individuals— but what prompts them to share ideas and concerns, contribute to one another's thinking, and warn the group early about potential risks is their connection to one another. Social capital lies at the heart of just cultures: it is what they depend on—and it is what they generate."[131]

As conventional hierarchies break down, social capital and informal networks have become a high priority. We are more interdependent on each other now than ever before. The real influencers are the network nodes: if you can't tap the right people for the right information, it's going to be difficult to do your job full stop. Leaders who are networked are at least three times more influential than people who aren't.

Knowledge networking is not just a leadership skill; it's about how you process information, make relationships, and get the job done. When you truly use networks, it changes the way you think. You plan and strategize differently.

## NAMES NOT NUMBERS

Julia Hobsbawm's impact on the practical study of knowledge networking has made her the world's first professor in networking and an honorary visiting professor at Cass Business School. She is the founder of Editorial Intelligence, a networking business committed to "developing deeper personal connections and having a more profound understanding of today's information overloaded landscape."

Her flagship event, Names Not Numbers (NNN), is an ideas festival where intellectually curious movers and shakers come together for learning and inspiration.

According to her latest research, 69.5 percent of survey respondents agree that "networking is essential for building and managing a career" and 53.3 percent strongly agree that "networking helps productivity because it brings fresh ideas and connections into the workplace." Hobsbawm says: "In big businesses I think we'll start to see chief networking officers alongside chief operating officers soon. They will be the dot-joiner-uppers of the corporate world. And it will feed into all elements of business. Networking can happen anywhere. You can make a connection with someone at a bus stop; either you can be that person who complains that a bus is late or say 'hi' to the person next to you and make a contact. You have to be curious. If you're not interested in anyone else and just want to shortcut in business, you're sunk."

How should you network smarter? A useful analogy is to imagine your own personal boardroom. Ask yourself "Who are the six to twelve individuals I need to build bridges with over time?" A simple knowledge dashboard is a useful way to stay ahead of the learning curve.

1. Watch (e.g., TED)
2. Hear (e.g., podcasts)
3. Read long (e.g., a *Harvard Business Review* article)
4. Read short (e.g., abstracts and summaries)
5. Read inspirational quotes (e.g., quote for your inner optimist)

## NEVER EAT ALONE

Marie Schneegans is the co-founder and CEO of a French startup, Never Eat Alone. The truth is, if you work in a large company, chances are you always eat alone at your desk or have lunch with the same people in your department. It's not easy to meet new people. This is a universal problem for thousands of people around the world: connections are missed, ideas are lost, and the work culture suffers as a result. Never Eat Alone puts an end to this. Its goal is to bring individuals together by using a customized lunch app on your phone. List your background and project interests and you can connect with colleagues who share similar goals. As an employee, you get to proactively reach out to anyone in the company, including the CEO, and for the organization, it's a great way to build a stronger whole-person culture where people bring more of themselves to work every day.

As social networking sites such as LinkedIn and Facebook take over the world, face-to-face contact is still of primary importance for leaders. A computer cannot trump the power of eye contact, tone of voice, and positive body language that can translate into strong working relationships between people. In a *Guardian* interview, Hobsbawm argues why face-to-face contact still matters: "People have been so obsessed with social networks that they really haven't noticed the human side, the non-algorithm side, is still where it's at."[132]

To learn fast, leaders use knowledge networking for three distinct reasons: the wisdom of crowds, reputation, and access.

## The Wisdom of Crowds

Y Combinator is a cluster of communities where collaborating is part of everything it does. If you're part of a group that has walked in your shoes before, it's incredibly reassuring to tap into the wisdom of the crowd. You can pull all these resources from your networks. That's going to give you the edge. In his personal blog, Y Combinator co-founder Sam Altman writes:

> Silicon Valley works because there is such a high density of people working on start-ups and they are inclined to help each other. Other tech hubs have this as well but this is a case of Metcalfe's law—the utility of a network is proportional to the square of the number of nodes on the network. Silicon Valley has far more nodes in the network than anywhere else.
>
> One of the biggest misconceptions about us is that you need to have pre-existing connections to get value from the network. Remarkably, you don't. Silicon Valley is a community of outsiders that have come together. If you build something good, people will help you. It's standard practice to ask people you've just met for help—and as long as you aren't annoying about it, they usually don't mind.[133]

Any company of more than 150 people can potentially feel like a "community of outsiders". For leaders, this can mean insufficient knowledge exchange and lack of interaction across the organization and for employees, there is little opportunity to meet colleagues from other departments. The challenge for every leader is to bring everyone together to build a community of insiders. Only then can you benefit from the wisdom of crowds.

## Reputation

Reputation tells others what to expect. As outdated command-and-control leadership styles become obsolete, becoming a "go-to" person should be at the top of every leader's agenda. This means building a reputation as someone whose actions match his words at every turn. We forget it all the time. Leaders own the trust and must earn it every day.

Networks can give you access to worlds you never knew existed. If you have access to diverse networks inside and outside your organization, the upside is considerable. Aside from influence, networks give you access to knowledge. They help you stay on top of new ideas and provide protection during a downturn. It's like having a safety net. If you fall, a strong network will catch you and enable you to recover more quickly.

Reputation matters. You have to be fully present and show gravitas, raising your game every day. In the war for talent, you must not only be smart but also *show* that you are smart.

## Access

Connection to others is as necessary as food, water, and shelter. Social media sites have all built their business models around the idea of social connection. In the book *Social: Why Our Brains Are Wired to Connect*, Matthew Lieberman, the renowned director of UCLA's Social Cognitive Neuroscience lab, explains that being socially connected is our brain's life-long passion. He writes: "Just as there are multiple social networks on the Internet such as Facebook and Twitter, each with its own strengths, there are also multiple social networks in our brains, sets of brain regions that work together to promote our social wellbeing. These networks each have their own strengths, and they have emerged at different points in our evolutionary history, moving from vertebrates to mammals to primates to us, *Homo sapiens*. Additionally, these same evolutionary steps are recapitulated in the same order during childhood."[134]

Strive to understand whether you and your team are fully connected.

- Have you built a culture of "we, not me"?
- Does your office environment and physical architecture support chance meetings?
- Is there a strong feeling of pride and community?
- Does collaboration get recognized and rewarded?
- Is connection valued in the company?

Community gives us a basic sense of worth. It's a pride builder. To feel part of something, the team and the vision are incredibly rewarding not just for our wellbeing but also for doing great work. Community comes from the Latin word *communus*, which means "shared gift". There is a growing body of research led by thinkers such as Wharton School professor Adam Grant that shows that collaboration is critical for reaching your leadership potential.

In his *New York Times* bestseller *Give and Take: Why Helping Others Drives Our Success*, Grant explores workplace dynamics and the value of collaboration. In a recent McKinsey interview, Grant elaborates: "All of these flattening structures, these ad hoc collaborations that require improvisation, are, at their core, about interdependence. And the data show that it's in interdependent situations that givers thrive. So if you're the kind of person who enjoys helping others, when you're working in a team, you have the ability to make the team better and really multiply the team's success in a way that, ideally, reverberates to benefit everyone in the team."[135]

Those with a leader's mindset put collaboration center stage in their organizations. In Morten Hansen's book *Collaboration*, he outlines how both weak ties and strong ties are necessary: "Research shows that it is not the size—the sheer number of contacts maintained by a person—that counts. Rather, it's the diversity of connections—the number of different types of people, units, expertise, technologies and viewpoints—that people can access through their networks."[136] Collaboration can spread high-performing behaviors throughout the organization.

To collaborate better, you must break through some cognitive biases that can derail your efforts. Three in particular must be understood in order to be more effective.

### Proximity Bias

Most office layouts create invisible walls of resistance for leaders. Today's work environment is often remote, with people working across different time zones and geographies. The proximity principle is an unconscious bias that influences who you spend the most time with and why. Simon Jones, a director of a global software company, says:

> You take for granted where you sit in the office. The truth is that it really matters. When I did an inventory of those whom I trusted the most, I found the majority of my relationships were within my own team and department. Do the test for yourself because it's a big wake-up call.
>
> My success depends on building bridges with people who sit mostly outside my department, such as Finance and HR. If you leave it to chance, you'll realize that the relationships that need building are the very ones that get neglected. Most leaders

are thinking 90 percent about their own agenda rather than the other person they are trying to connect with. It makes the job more difficult trying to influence a stranger.

A question many leaders ask is how long to spend on knowledge networking. The answer is: more than you are spending today. A minimum of two hours a week of intelligent networking is a sensible starting point. Have a plan: make a list of whom you know and whom you need to know. Use a simple trust index to capture the biggest trust gaps within the organization. This works by assessing what you believe to be the relative levels of trust held between you and your colleagues on a scale of 1–10. The biggest gaps demand more attention.

Collaborating with others doesn't happen overnight. It's a long-term campaign, but the effort is well worth it. Jones continues:

> Find a reason to say hello and grab a coffee. Having a strong network means being able to ask for help but also offering it. If you're invisible you won't even figure on the other person's radar. That's a problem because most of your success will be based on IWA skills (Influencing Without Authority).
>
> Look for areas of mutual interest. What I do is allocate a few hours a week to connect, growing a wide selection of contacts across the company. That includes vertically and horizontally. Once a week I like to sit in a different department alongside some new folks. You have to take a strategic approach and be ready to play the long game. Finally, you must show a genuine interest in helping that person progress and respect their time.

Take action to make knowledge networking part of your everyday mindset. The key is to build a wide pool of networks across functions, industries, and experiences—diversity is key.

### The Self-Similarity Bias

Try this test: make a list of the ten most important people in your network. Chances are they'll be similar to you in many ways, including in their experience level, education, perspective, status, and values. Don't worry, this is perfectly normal—it's called the self-similarity principle. We mostly hang out with people of similar tastes and backgrounds. The problem is that too much similarity in your networks restricts your access to different perspectives, which are vital for creativity and problem solving. It becomes a constraint to thinking differently and can lead to blind spots in the company that go unnoticed until they become a crisis.

In a *Forbes* interview, David Rock, the founder of the Neuroleadership Institute, says: "We've evolved to put people in our in-group and out-group. We put most people in our out-group and a few people in our in-group. It determines whether we care about others. It determines whether we support or attack them. The process is a byproduct of our evolutionary history where we lived in small groups and strangers we didn't know well weren't to be trusted."[137] The default setting for most leaders is closed networks where you are connected to people who already know each other. To combat the self-similarity bias, leaders should take an audit of who's in their in-group and out-group, and then act upon the results.

### HiPPOs

Hierarchy and ego are some of the biggest obstacles to collaborating, as evidenced by the "HiPPO bias". "HiPPO" stands for the "highest-paid person's opinion" and describes the tendency for lower-paid employees to always agree with a HiPPO. This can happen at a conference, a meeting, or even the boardroom. In *How Google Works*, authors Eric Schmidt and Jonathan Rosenberg write: "Hippopotamuses are among the deadliest animals, faster than you think and capable of crushing (or biting in half) any enemy in their path. Hippos are dangerous in companies too."[138]

It's human nature to put others on pedestals, especially where power, status, and money are concerned. I once came across a director whose nickname in private circles was "the shark of sharks". Needless to say, when he held meetings there was only one opinion in the room that counted.

The HiPPO bias can have some nasty side effects: good ideas get ignored because of someone's job title. Those whose opinions are never challenged run the risk of egoism, and their sense of reality can become distorted.

The global financial crisis of 2007 happened for many reasons; however, there's no question that too many companies decided to follow their HiPPOs rather than make a stand—Royal Bank of Scotland, Arthur Andersen, and Lehman Brothers come to mind. The longer we lead, the more difficult it is to remain objective; we get sucked into the day to day, where our default setting can become tunnel vision.

To overcome the curse of HiPPO bias in your own company, you must conquer the self-imposter syndrome. This unhelpful mindset occurs when you're in a room and the little guy inside your head is talking you down: *I'm out of my league here. Everyone knows more than me. That's a dumb question to ask.* Everyone has a duty to stand up and be heard—express an idea, ask an opinion, or raise a fear. Listen to your gut and have the courage to speak up.

The onus is on all of us to lead by example. If you're the highest-paid person in the room, let others speak first, and thank them when they offer a new opinion.

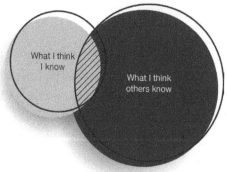

*The Self-Imposter Syndrome*

The two-pizza rule, often credited to Amazon CEO Jeff Bezos, is a simple idea for managing HiPPOs: no meeting should have more than enough attendees for two large pizzas. For argument's sake, this limits the number to no more than eight attendees. Putting a limit on the number of attendees in a meeting can help reduce HiPPOs and their close relative, groupthink, the bias that makes us agree with everyone else for fear of being seen as an outsider.

## GROUPTHINK

Solomon Asch's conformity experiments in the 1950s offer a strong lesson in the power of groupthink. Asch gave his participants the following task: pick which of three different lines—A, B, or C—was most like the target line. The task was obvious, but there was a catch: out of eight people, only one was a genuine subject and the other seven were close associates of Asch's who had been instructed to unanimously pick a line that did not match.

The questions were "Would the subject stick to their guns and trust their own eyes?" and "Would they be swayed by group pressure and conform to the majority view?"

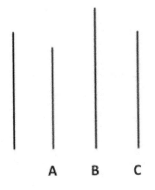

A    B    C

*The Asch Experiment*

### The Asch Experiment

Asch measured the number of times the subject conformed to the majority view. On average, about a third of the subjects gave in to groupthink, even when the answer was clearly wrong (C was the correct answer). Over all the trials, about 75 percent of subjects conformed at least once to the incorrect answer and only 25 percent of subjects never conformed.[139]

Why did so many of the subjects doubt their own eyes and agree with the rest of the group? Offered a choice between speaking our mind and fitting in with the group, we opt for fitting into the group almost every time. Social pressure matters more than we imagine it does. We also assume that the group is better informed than us even when the truth is clear to see. There's nothing more dangerous than a group of minds that are too afraid to tell the truth. Do you have an ideas-led culture or hierarchy-led culture? To defeat groupthink, you must put measures in place that reward dissent and encourage straight talking at all levels. Having a contrarian in the team is a good idea.

### Dunbar's Number

The number 150 is significant for anyone who wants to get ahead in business. It can help you decide where to focus your attention and on whom.

Robin Dunbar is the director of the Institute of Cognitive and Evolutionary Anthropology at Oxford University and the author of *How Many Friends Does One Person Need?* He has spent more than twenty years studying social behavior and has found that 150 is the optimal number or anthropological limit for the number of meaningful relationships we can have.

Dunbar noticed that most tribes have around 150 members, and even armies throughout Western history, from the Roman Empire to the modern-day US military, have around 150 soldiers in a small company.

In an interview in the *Guardian*, he says: "The way in which our social world is constructed is part and parcel of our biological inheritance. Together with apes and monkeys, we're members of the primate family—and within primates there is a general relationship between the size of the brain and the size of the social group. We fit in a pattern. There are social circles beyond it and layers within—but there is a natural grouping of 150. This is the number of people you can have a relationship with involving trust and obligation—there's some personal history, not just names and faces."[140]

As with any human trait, there will always be outliers—those who have the capacity to know a lot more people. Now with the advent of social media sites such as Instagram, it's possible to connect to hundreds if not thousands of people.

However, it's face-to-face contact where the highest exchanges of trust and respect occur. Dunbar's number can help you organize your connecting and collaborating efforts in a more systematic way, saving time and energy:

- Make a list of the key people in your organization—that is, those whom you depend on the most to get the job done.
- Prioritize them in order of importance.
- Find a mutually beneficial reason to connect.
- Reach out to them.
- Sustain your relationships for the long term.

## Knowledge Circles

In June 2013, the Massachusetts Institute of Technology (MIT) invited Drew Houston, the CEO and founder of Dropbox, to speak at its annual commencement ceremonies. Houston, a former MIT student, gave this advice:

> They say that you're the average of the five people you spend the most time with. Think about that for a minute: who would be in your circle of five? I have some good news: MIT is one of the best places in the world to start building that circle. If I hadn't come here, I wouldn't have met Adam, I wouldn't have met my amazing cofounder, Arash, and there would be no Dropbox.

One thing I've learned is surrounding yourself with inspiring people is now just as important as being talented or working hard. Can you imagine if Michael Jordan hadn't been in the NBA, if his circle of five had been a bunch of guys in Italy? Your circle pushes you to be better, just as Adam pushed me. And now your circle will grow to include coworkers and everyone around you. Meeting my heroes and learning from them gave me a huge advantage. Your heroes are part of your circle too—follow them. If the real action is happening somewhere else, move.[141]

One of your biggest priorities as a leader is to build knowledge circles inside and outside of your organization. Knowledge circles are inspired by the creative circles of the French post-impressionists, known as the Société des Artistes Indépendants. Famous artists such as Paul Cezanne, Vincent van Gogh, and Georges Seurat came together at cafés in the Parisian suburb of Montparnasse to connect, share ideas, and draw upon the wisdom of their peers. Heated debates and even drunken brawls occasionally spilled out onto the street. While I do not condone drunken brawling, I do believe that leaders can be more creative by embracing new experiences, breaking out of old patterns, and stepping into the shoes of others more.

In an exclusive *Wired* interview, Steve Jobs expounded on some of the principles of Société des Artistes Indépendants:

Creativity is just connecting things. When you ask creative people how they did something, they feel a little guilty, because they didn't really do it, they just saw something. It seemed obvious to them after a while. That's because they were able to connect experiences they've had and synthesize new things. And the reason they were able to do that was that they've had more experiences or they have thought more about their experiences than other people. A lot of people in our industry haven't had very diverse experiences, so they don't have enough dots to connect, and they end up with very linear solutions without a broad perspective on the problem. The broader one's understanding of the human experience, the better design we will have.[142]

To think more creatively, don't be afraid to broaden your experiences and welcome different and even opposing opinions and viewpoints. This will ensure that your mindset doesn't become fixed or worse, stuck in the past.

Here are four knowledge circles to build:

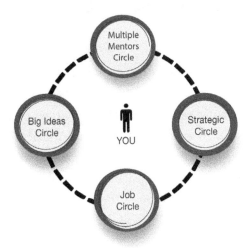

*The Leader's Orbit*

## Multiple Mentors Circle

Build up a pool of mentors, both inside and outside of your organization. Face-to-face contact works best, although this isn't always necessary with the advent of Skype and other technologies. When approaching a potential mentor, be specific with your request for guidance and agree to the frequency of meetings and outcomes at the outset.

A good rule of thumb is to meet once a quarter for forty-five minutes with some clear, actionable points to take away. Even if you meet just once it's better than nothing.

One leader, whom I interviewed, shares her story: "For me it's about throwing out the rulebook on mentors. Your network is your new mentor. It's about being able to ask for help. The worst that can happen is that you don't get a reply. Anyone can do it."

A shortcut is to ask a mentor to suggest other people who may be able to help in specific areas. Having multiple mentors is by far one of the most effective ways to accelerate your growth. Approach people with a goal and you'll be surprised at how many say yes; just don't waste their time. Be crystal clear about your "why" before introducing yourself.

## Strategic Circle

A strategic circle is made up of thinkers who hold expert status in your industry. They could sit inside and outside of your organization. They have built up a profile as opinion leaders whose opinion counts; this means that what they say directly impacts your operating environment, how your business runs, or even industry regulations. They may not be in your immediate circle but will exert considerable power over how things get done. They could be leaders, competitors, or even your own boss. It's useful to connect to these people on LinkedIn and Twitter. Distill the views of each thinker and use them to build up a rich context about the type of world you're operating in today.

We are usually adept at the operational side of work—after all, that's where we spend most of our time. But what's got you to where you are won't get you to where you want to be. You have to have an eye on the future as well; this is the big picture as well as the detail. Your strategic circle will give you access to the type of information, trends, and insights that your future self will thank you for.

## Operational Circle (Job)

The operational circle is where we spend most of our time. It's the job—this means our immediate boss, their boss, and our team. This is our inner circle, where success will depend on the help of others. Trust is key, as power structure and organizational structure are very different.

Other departments will also fit within the operational circle: human resources, finance, marketing, and information technology. We should reach out to those we depend on—an informal coffee together to check in for fifteen minutes builds goodwill and strengthens the relationship. Job rotation, cross-functional projects, and sitting with another team for half a day are proven ways to sharpen your operational circle, and stay connected to people and ideas.

## Big Ideas Circle

This is like your very own panel of pioneers and experimentalists. It is made up of people who send an electric jolt to your brain when they speak.

The big ideas circle is curiosity driven and lives in the future. The individuals who occupy it are those such as coveted scientists, writers, painters, anthropologists, and economists. You may not get to meet them in person, but you can certainly get closer to them. Follow them on Twitter, watch them on TED, attend an ideas conference, and read their articles and books. The big ideas circle should be wide and diverse like a "latticework of connections," says Charlie Munger, the billionaire business partner of Warren Buffett.

## GOOD MENTORS RAISE YOUR GAME

Aaron Levie is a big fan of reaching out to mentors. He is the twentysomething CEO of Box, the leading enterprise tech company that opened on the NYSE with a market cap of nearly $3 billion.[143] In the early years, before setting up Box, Levie worked hard to find mentors and big-name leaders for advice. *ReadWrite* editor-in-chief Dan Lyons sat down with him to discuss his journey from rookie to leader. Levie says:

> There's no risk in somebody not responding to your email. The cool thing about Silicon Valley—and this is something that is remarkable about this ecosystem—is the mentorship network, the appreciation I think everybody has for the fight and struggle of building companies. I've benefited greatly from people who had built enterprise software companies or just big companies in general, and they were very helpful in the kind of things we should watch out for, the kind of things we should optimize for, and how to build an organization that can last as long as possible.[144]

Good mentors can raise their protégés' game as well as build a stronger talent pipeline. Warren Buffett is a notable mentor to Bill Gates, while Marissa Mayer, CEO of Yahoo, credits Eric Roberts, her former science professor at Stanford University, and Google's Larry Page as her mentors. When Steve Jobs passed away, Mark Zuckerberg of Facebook acknowledged that the Apple founder had been an "incredibly important mentor."[145]

Why learn from your own mistakes in business when you can learn from someone else's? Mentors are indispensable: they provide the insights we are missing and open doors to new connections that might otherwise take years to build. With the meteoric pace of change, it's essential for leaders to have a private space to reflect and talk through challenges they face. Rockstar Mentoring Group, for instance, aims to provide that and is blazing a trail in the world of startups. Founded by Jonathan Pfahl, an ex–Goldman Sachs wealth manager, Rockstar has built a reputation for accelerating leadership success for others.

A good mentor will help you bolster self-awareness and emotional intelligence—two vital leadership qualities. Every leader has a blind spot, visible to others but not to themselves. Mentors will help you see your blind spot and also give feedback so that you're always thinking about what you can do better.

I'd estimate that around 75 percent of leaders use or plan to use a mentor at some stage. They understand the benefits of working with a mentor. Jack Dorsey, CEO of Square and cofounder of Twitter, credits philanthropist Ray Chambers as one of his closet mentors. A feature in *Business Insider* states that Chambers has said: "Dorsey has learned to think bigger and better from Chambers and 'at the core of his being, he really wants to make the world a better place.'"[146]

A mentor's track record counts for everything. Check your mentor's history to see that he or she will bring new learning into the mentoring relationship. And don't restrict a mentor to just one. Go for multiple mentors. In a *Forbes* interview, LinkedIn CEO Reid Hoffman concludes:

I don't have one mentor. My network mentors me. I have different mentors on different subjects. Part of how I parse the world is that different people have different expertise that I can massively learn from. If I want the perspective of someone who has had amazing growth from being young into being a totally hitting CEO, I go to [Mark] Zuckerberg. For understanding the software development world, including open-source, John Lilly, the former CEO of Mozilla who is now [a venture partner] at Greylock. On virality, Greg Tseng, the founder/

CEO of Tagged, and his partner Johann Schleier-Smith. On understanding enterprise software, Aneel Bhusri, a partner here [at Greylock]. The list goes on. So it's not one mentor. It's a constellation, a network of mentors who really amplify my abilities and knowledge in particular vectors.[147]

In my own company, I've been mentoring a young entrepreneur who recently raised $1.5 million for his own startup and was named in the *Forbes* "30 under 30" list. I also serve as a mentor for Future Ideas, a global community made up of top minds, including the *New York Times*–bestselling author Daniel Pink; Stewart Friedman, professor of management at the University of Pennsylvania; and Richard Florida of the University of Toronto's Rotman School of Management.

The goal of Future Ideas (www.futureideas.org) is to connect "the best ideas with innovators and entrepreneurs round the world." Every year, its worldwide Academic Competition is launched to find the most radical thinking in business. Six themes are covered, including the future of business, the future of community, and the future of technology. Students submit their best ideas, and the winner for each theme receives a cash prize and worthwhile mentorship from the Future Ideas community.

Future Ideas is one example of a fast-growing mentoring platform on which entrepreneurs can receive vital learning and support. People simply won't try if the fear of failure is too high. I believe a society that encourages risk taking will fundamentally be a wealthier one, too.

## THE NEW SCIENCE OF TEAMWORK

Most teams are not teams. They are just groups of individuals without a single collective purpose. Teamwork is fundamental for success in any organization, yet most teams struggle to cooperate over long periods and fall into dysfunctional behaviors and personality clashes. Patrick Lencioni, in his bestseller *The Five Dysfunctions of a Team*, identified five gaps that impede most teams: absence of trust, fear of conflict, lack of commitment, avoidance of accountability, and inattention to results.

Smart teamwork requires a team mindset known as collective intelligence. As the name implies, collective intelligence arises when groups work together to be smarter and perform better; it's the team capacity for high performance. Thomas W. Malone is a professor of management at the MIT Sloan School of Management and a founding director of the MIT Center for Collective Intelligence. The center's mission is "to understand collective intelligence at a deep level so we can create and take advantage of the new possibilities it enables."[148]

Faculty members are drawn from many different parts of MIT, including the Media Lab, the Department of Brain and Cognitive Sciences, and the Computer Science and Artificial Intelligence Lab. Their aim is to identify what makes some teams smarter than others. What does it take to tap the collective intelligence of your own team, and how can leaders do that? Malone and a team of MIT researchers studied a raft of factors, such as psychological safety, personality types, and gender that turn a group into a smart, high-performing team.

In two studies, published in 2010 in the journal *Science*, researchers grouped 697 volunteers into teams of two to five members. Each team was required to work together to complete a range of cognitive tasks, from brainstorming to teamwork and problem solving. What they found was that individual intelligence (as measured by IQ) was not as important as they had assumed. Nor did teams with more extroverted people or individual stars make a noticeable difference to the group's overall success. What did matter was empathy, the ability to read others' emotions, and frequent communication with equal respect for each team member's opinion.

Writing in the *New York Times*, Malone discussed his findings:

Instead, the smartest teams were distinguished by three characteristics: First, their members contributed more equally to the team's discussion, rather than letting one or two people dominate the group. Second, their members scored higher on a test called Reading the Mind in the Eyes, which measures how well people can read complex emotional states from images of faces with only the eyes visible. Finally, teams with more women outperformed teams with more men. Indeed, it appeared that it was not "diversity" (having equal numbers of men and women) that mattered for a team's intelligence, but simply having more women. This last effect, however, was partly explained by the fact that women, on average, were better at "mindreading" than men.[149]

Collective intelligence cuts to the heart of Formula One. This hyper competitive sport is all about winning and is a great example to other sports (and industries) that aspire to reach the top of their game. Every week the drivers test the limits of human and super-car performance around the track. The pressure is intense and unrelenting. More than 1,000 data points in the car are analyzed during a race, helping to improve every time-sensitive aspect of the car. Few teams have dominated F1 like the Mercedes AMG Petronas Formula One Team headed up by the Austrian, Torger Christian "Toto" Wolff. In the last three years alone, they have built some of the fastest cars in Grand Prix history. F1 Champion Lewis Hamilton won the world championship in 2015 and is a favorite to win again.

To understand the secret of Mercedes's success in F1, you must understand the culture—the way it does things. It's in the DNA of everything it does. Based in Brackley, England, the sense of purpose and clarity is electric. In an exclusive interview with Matthew Syed of *The Times* newspaper, technical head Paddy Lowe says: "F1 is an unusual environment because you have incredibly smart people driven by the desire to win. The ambition spurs rapid innovation. Things from just two years ago seem antique. Standing still is tantamount to extinction."[150]

At Mercedes, purpose is the difference that makes the difference.

Like Mercedes, the McLaren F1 Team is a byword for focus and uncompromising teamwork. With Ron Dennis at the helm as group CEO and Eric Boullier taking over from Martin Whitmarsh as team principal, it has an unrelenting desire to win. Since arriving in the sport in 1996, it has won more Grand Prix races than any other Formula 1 team. Quite simply, McLaren exists to win.

The headquarters, nestled in the English countryside, is a showcase for excellence. There's a high performing building designed by the world-renowned architects Foster + Partners. Most office buildings undermine teamwork: low ceilings, poor artificial light, and physical silos on different floors render most teams fragmented and lacking the type of unity required to win.

McLaren F1 stands out in a world where most companies are trapped in traditional twentieth-century mindsets. Its headquarters has plenty of natural light, open spaces, and thirty-foot floor-to-ceiling windows that you'd expect to find in luxury apartments overlooking New York's Central Park. Outside there's woodland for informative "walk and talk" meetings and even a lake to help busy minds unplug. The whole building is designed to encourage tightly knit collaboration: everyone must understand their roles and others' expansively and work as one team with a clear, nonnegotiable common goal. It's all about making crystal clear choices about focus, clear choices about priorities, and clear choices about what needs to change in order to reach the destination.

Building collective intelligence in teams sounds like an abstract idea, but it derives from some deliberate actions. Take time to measure how many of the above steps you follow and know that investment in time and effort will be worthwhile.

To grow your own team, do these actions:

1. **Face to face** really does count, whether you're working online or offline. This is known as the theory of mind—it's the ability to show deep empathy, passion, and compassion and to appreciate what others think, feel, and believe. Look for face time opportunities in your schedule and override your default setting to use email all the time. Use different environments to keep the conversations alive—it's also a useful safeguard against lazy, unproductive habits.

2. **Communication** using different channels builds up the all-important social capital, which binds a team together emotionally and psychologically. This strengthens mutual trust and sharpens emotion-reading skills for the whole team. Imagine social capital as a bank where you make regular credits and debits. Without it, you don't get the tough debates that problems demand and the fresh ideas and new perspectives that will propel a company forward. Not speaking speaks volumes. Y Combinator has adopted the Japanese principle of *ba*—to get involved and transcend one's own limited perspective or boundary. Put another way, *ba* refers to a physical, virtual, or mental space shared by two or more individuals. You can unlock the intelligence embedded in *ba* by providing diverse meeting spaces and the creative freedom to unshackle from boring routines.

3. **Equal participation,** the opportunity to have a voice and be heard even when there is a dissenting view, is mandatory for respect and a willingness to help each other. Job titles, hierarchy, and self-imposter syndrome are just some of the

barriers that prevent equal participation and can only be overcome with perseverance. In a recent entrepreneurship talk at the Stanford School of Engineering, XSeed Capital partner Alan Chiu emphasized the power of collective intelligence: "Winning teams pull together people with complementary strengths. Everyone is the center of their own universe. By empathizing with another person's stress, pain, and fear, you'll be more effective in understanding what you need to do to help that teammate be more successful. Connecting with the other person's universe can even open up additional opportunities for you. Who wouldn't want to work with someone who consistently helps make them successful?"[151]

## SPEAK UP!

Getspeakup is a new idea to tap the collective intelligence of teams. Three years ago, Ray Gillenwater had a $500,000 high-flying job at Blackberry. But he decided to quit and follow his passion to bootstrap a new startup called Getspeakup. In an interview with *Business Insider*, he tells his story: "Most companies are bad at upward communication. A lot are good at top-to-bottom style communication, the kind the military invented, but very rarely is a company good at extracting insight from employees who know the company and its customers best."[152]

Many leaders are still doing things the old way using twentieth-century boss-and-control models like a general on the battlefield. Opportunities are missed, conversations are wasted, and teams become invisible. The leader's mindset is different. It places a huge amount of value on talent and ideas, always looking for better ways to extract the best thinking and creativity from others.

Getspeakup encourages collective intelligence by giving everyone equal participation and a voice in the direction of the company. Teams share ideas and chats across functions, geography, and time zones, which is incredibly empowering for everyone. One of the most frustrating parts of anyone's career is trying to cut through all the corporate layers and channels to communicate ideas and problems to the actual decision maker. For many people, there are an unconscionable number of obstacles to overcome in order to have a voice and be heard.

Another perk is less wasted time in meetings, one of the biggest demotivators for most teams. Decision making is faster, and communication is more efficient. Leaders must use collective intelligence and know it's one of their biggest sources of competitive advantage. The alternative is collective stupidity and wasted talent.

## NEVER STOP LEARNING

Learn fast (Knowledge Seeker) is the final mindset to 10X and is one that requires daily commitment. Step outside your normal circle and meet someone new with a different background than your own. This is based upon the ancient Chinese proverb "A single conversation across the table with a wise man is worth a month's study of books." Travel to an unfamiliar destination. Attend a great talk or even watch one on TED. Have a curiosity for new experiences and never stop learning. Researcher Liz Wiseman says: "If you are at the top of your game, it might be time to position yourself at the bottom of the learning curve."[153]

One of my favorite stories of learning comes from a delightful lady named Doreetha Daniels, who at the age of ninety-nine achieved her personal goal of earning a college degree. Ever since she was very young, she'd dreamed of going to college. The truth is that our parents' and grandparents' generations had less opportunity than ours. For many, it was simply about survival, having to contend with two world wars and supporting large, young families.

Times have changed, and Daniels's thirst for learning is an inspiration to everyone, young and old. When her grandchildren got their master's degrees, she pledged to herself and her family that she'd graduate college before she turned one hundred. During her studies, she lost her driver's license and even suffered two strokes. However, her strong spirit and sunny outlook saw her through, and in 2015, she fulfilled her lifelong dream of earning a degree before turning one hundred. She was quoted on *BET*'s National News website: "Don't give up. Do it. Don't let anybody discourage you… Say that, 'I'm going to do it,' and do it for yourself."[154]

In the final chapter, we look at the best hacks and shortcuts to sustain the leader's mindset for the long haul.

## CHAPTER 5

# FINAL THOUGHTS, HACKS, AND SHORTCUTS

*"Achievement is talent plus preparation."*
— **Malcolm Gladwell**

## MAKE YOUR OWN LUCK

According to Joel Brown, entrepreneur and cofounder of Impact Billions, a global movement for changing lives, only one in ten leaders who announce their New Year's resolutions will have stuck with them after January.

We've all been there, brimming with optimism at the start of our resolution but then giving up even though fulfilling the resolution would have improved our lives.

We tend to associate luck with superstition or strange forces outside our control. It's probably time to challenge this outdated way of thinking. Tina Seeling, executive director of the Stanford Technology Ventures program and author of *What I Wish I Knew When I Was 20*, writes:

"Lucky people don't just pay attention to the world around them and meet interesting individuals—they also find unusual ways to use and recombine their knowledge and experiences. Most people have remarkable resources at their fingertips, but never figure out how to leverage them. However, lucky people appreciate the value of their knowledge and their network, and tap into their goldmines as needed." Leaders who feel lucky report higher levels of motivation and wellbeing, both essential for sustaining performance during tough times. So how do you cultivate your own daily luck?[155]

*The Luck Quotient*

Luck is a skill that can be developed. It's about a flexibility of mind and a willingness to listen to your heart and trust your gut. Take advantage of chance occurrences, break the weekly routine, and once in a while have the courage to let go. The world is full of opportunity if you're prepared to embrace it. Steve Jobs emphasized the importance of trusting your gut when he delivered his now infamous commencement address at Stanford University:

> If I had never dropped out, I would have never dropped in on this calligraphy class, and personal computers might not have the wonderful typography that they do. Of course it was impossible to connect the dots looking forward when I was in college. But it was very, very clear looking backwards ten years later. Again, you can't connect the dots looking forward;

you can only connect them looking backwards. So you have to trust that the dots will somehow connect in your future. You have to trust in something—your gut, destiny, life, and karma, whatever. This approach has never let me down, and it has made all the difference in my life.[156]

Luck is as much about what you expect as what you do. Do you wait for success to happen, or do you get out there and make it happen?

In his book *The Luck Factor*, Professor Richard Wiseman of the University of Hertfordshire, England, describes why lucky people tend to share traits that make them luckier than others. This includes the impact of chance opportunities, lucky breaks, and being in the right place at the right time. In an interview with the *Telegraph*, he says: "My research revealed that lucky people generate good fortune via four basic principles. They are skilled at creating and noticing chance opportunities, make lucky decisions by listening to their intuition, create self-fulfilling prophesies via positive expectations, and adopt a resilient attitude that transforms bad luck into good." On the flipside he says: "Those who think they're unlucky should change their outlook and discover how to generate good fortune."[157]

## THE LUCK PROJECT

One of Wiseman's most famous studies examined why some people are luckier than others and how to increase your luck quotient in life. The results were surprising. He writes: "Ten years ago I decided to take a more scientific investigation into the concept of luck. I decided that the best method was to examine why some people are consistently lucky whilst others encounter little but ill fortune. In short, why some people seem to live charmed lives full of lucky breaks and chance encounters, while others experience one disaster after another."[158]

Wiseman placed advertisements in the press asking readers who thought of themselves as lucky or unlucky to contact him. They came from all walks of life, from a graduate to a CEO. All agreed to let him study their lives to understand if there is such a thing as a luck quotient that we can control. Over the course of a month he asked volunteers to follow daily exercises that could help them build up a lucky mindset. These exercises included breaking with routine, trying something new, expecting to be lucky, and being more resilient in the face of bad luck.

At the end of the experiment he found that 80 percent of volunteers felt more optimistic about the future and, most critically, felt luckier. Wiseman continues: "The findings have revealed that luck is not a magical ability or the result of random chance. Nor are people born lucky or unlucky. Instead, although lucky people and unlucky people have almost no insight into the real causes of their good and bad luck, their thoughts and behavior are responsible for much of their fortune."[159]

The study showed that to a large extent, people make their own good and bad fortune and that it is possible to enhance the amount of luck that people encounter in their lives. In the *Telegraph* interview Wiseman says: "Unlucky people often fail to follow their intuition when making a choice, whereas lucky people tend to respect hunches. Lucky people are interested in how they both think and feel about the various options, rather than simply looking at the rational side of the situation. I think this helps them because gut feelings act as an alarm bell—a reason to consider a decision carefully."[160]

You can grow your luck quotient by being forward looking, buoyant, and more proactive as a leader. Wiseman concludes: "Personality tests revealed that unlucky people are generally much more tense and anxious than lucky people, and research has shown that anxiety disrupts people's ability to notice the unexpected."[161]

Take the initiative and do something new every day. The self-similarity principle draws us towards like-minded people who share similar values and mindsets about the world. While this is a comfortable default setting it can also lead to groupthink and less opportunity to explore new thinking, essential for the leader's mindset. One of the biggest enemies of luck is routine and boredom. I agree with Nobel Prize–winning biochemist Albert Szent-Györgyi, who says "A discovery is said to be an accident meeting a prepared mind."[162]

## OWN WHO YOU ARE

Sahar Hashemi epitomizes the make-your-own-luck mindset. She is one of the United Kingdom's best-known female entrepreneurs and is behind success stories such as Coffee Republic, the coffee bar chain, and Skinny Candy, the guilt-free confectionery brand. After studying law at Bristol University in the UK, Hashemi became a practicing lawyer but knew early on that something was missing in her life. In many companies, it's still the norm to not bring 100 percent of yourself to work every day—millions of people "quit and stay" by mentally quitting the job but remaining at the company to collect a paycheck. Hashemi, however, could not accept the idea that this was her fate, to remain unfulfilled and be unable to be herself and express her own individuality.

After five years working as a lawyer, Hashemi's world shattered when tragedy struck the family. Her father, who had been fit and healthy, suddenly died from a stroke. For Hashemi, who had been part of a loving, close-knit family, the death was devastating. It forced her to question the fragility of life and the whole idea of a comfort zone, which often imprisons us. One year after her father passed away, Hashemi bravely decided to give up the security of her lawyer job and take a leap of faith into the unknown. She took some time to visit her brother, Bobby Hashemi, who was an investment banker living in New York.

Arriving in the big city, jetlagged, she strolled down Madison Avenue in search of a caffeine fix. At the time, coffee bars did not exist in the UK, so it was a real treat to discover New World Coffee, a busy coffee bar with freshly ground coffee beans and delicious double chocolate muffins. On returning to the UK, Hashemi missed the great coffee she'd stumbled across in New York. A lightbulb came on: there simply were no coffee bars in London, so there was room to establish them there. Without a job and uncertain of what the future held, Hashemi's brother challenged her to research her "coffee bar in the UK" idea to see if it had potential.

The dial had been set. Without any prior knowledge of coffee or the catering industry, Hashemi researched the London coffee bar market. Her approach was elegantly simple. I call it the "secret squirrel strategy", whereby you get out there and mystery shop the competition. As legend goes, Hashemi used the famous London tube map, stopping at each of the twenty-seven stations on the Circle Line to answer one question: "Do coffee bars exist in London?" She quickly reached the conclusion that they didn't.

It became clear to Hashemi that her window of opportunity wouldn't be open for long. Knowing how quickly coffee bars had taken off in the United States, she realized it would only be a matter of months before someone brought them to the UK—if she didn't do it first. Hashemi and her brother made a bold decision: they would join forces to set up the UK's first chain of coffee bars. Hashemi, speaking at a TEDx conference, says: "Leap and the net will appear. We will always battle it out with the two sides of our brain, creativity on the right, and rationality on the left. Sometimes one just has to hit the delete button when the voice of fear tries to take over. The left brain stops innovation."[163] Sometimes, as a leader you have to do more and doubt less—quickly. If you wait for perfection, opportunities are lost forever.

Being clueless is one of Hashemi's most famous principles, reminding leaders that sometimes naivety can be a gift, especially when companies are seeking faster, better, or cheaper ways of doing things. She writes: "Your skills, experience and how we've always done it mentality will blind you from seeing new opportunities. Break from established thinking and un-learn so you stumble on new ways of doing things."[164] One of the biggest enemies of innovation is inertia, when leaders lose their impatience to change or take a risk. This is particularly true for large, successful companies that become victims of their own success: they get bigger and more scared of making mistakes. They stop innovating, which is the lifeblood of any company.

Next, Hashemi and her brother had to secure funding to set up the first coffee shop. They had a problem though: the UK is known as a nation of tea drinkers, so bank managers simply did not believe that coffee bars would ever take off in the UK. Hashemi contacted more than forty bank managers and secured meetings with twenty, of which nineteen flatly rejected her idea.

She writes: "Accept that there is a status quo bias and new ways of doing things (however great) always meet with resistance. Never stop at a 'no,' it's just someone's opinion. Famous people we all know have notched up hundreds of nos. Starbucks CEO Howard Schultz was famously rejected 278 times before getting a yes."[165]

Hashemi's resolute self-belief and enthusiasm finally paid off: in her last meeting, she finally raised the funding to open her first Coffee Republic shop. It was not an overnight success. On opening day, it remained mostly empty, apart from Hashemi's loyal mother, who dutifully drank multiple cups of coffee. Achievers do what it takes and understand that overnight success is a fallacy: in reality it takes many years and hard work to become an overnight success. After six months, Coffee Republic broke even, and its fortunes began to improve every day.

After the first coffee bar, expansion happened quickly, and Coffee Republic grew to become a major player within a few years. Hashemi credits bootstrapping as a skill for developing a leader's mindset. "Bootstrapping is about somehow making 2+2=5 by making the most of what you've got. Entrepreneurs are forced to bootstrap because of scarcity of resources. So big companies don't bootstrap. But this is a good discipline to instill in large companies. It adds momentum and it's a way of getting round corporate traffic jams that stall new initiatives."[166]

At its height, Coffee Republic had over 110 stores and a turnover of $45 million before being taken over by investors. As the UK's first national coffee brand, Hashemi and her brother had to notch up many nos to turn their idea into reality. There will always be the doomsters whose job in life is to stop you from reaching your goals. If you have a clear vision and love what you do, you just don't give up easily—nor should you.

Hashemi's story began as a giant leap into the dark. She says: "We knew nothing about coffee and were blissfully unaware of the obstacles. Not having experience can be one of your greatest advantages."[167] The leader's mindset must decide faster in the age of disruption. It doesn't just see the future, it seizes it, accepting an outsized appetite for risk and the unknown as part of the journey.

## PREPARE YOUR BRAIN FOR CHANGE

Try this exercise, which will take less than a minute: the Apple logo is one of the most recognized and iconic in the world. It is bold and distinct—one of the best in modern design. It's quite likely you own an Apple product or know somebody who does. We see the logo all the time, but do we remember it? If I asked you how confident you are at drawing the Apple logo, how would you reply? Confident? Without peeking, draw the logo. (If you prefer, you can do the challenge online at http://gnodevel.ugent.be/memory-logo). Now check your drawing with the official Apple logo. How did you do?

In a study on attention and recall featured in the *Quarterly Journal of Experimental Psychology*, researchers found that only one out of eighty-five participants could recall the logo without any errors.

There was a striking difference between participants' confidence levels before the test and the actual results.[168] I was surprised when I got it wrong, too.

You can spend more time growing your company and developing your talent if you remove the barriers to being effective. Uber CEO Travis Kalanick says: "I want to do one thing only, and do it really well." Kalanick is a master at removing interference and getting things done. Find out what's keeping you from doing your best work and remove it.

Here are five hacks to use.

### Stop Managing Time, Start Managing Focus

Leaders are under pressure to do things more quickly with ever-diminishing attention spans, and many work hard to answer every request as fast as possible. And though the cell phone is by far one of the best inventions of the last century, I believe it is also one of the biggest threats to harnessing a leader's mindset. There are only 480 minutes in an eight-hour workday: focus matters.

Busy leaders are prone to a false sense of urgency reacting to emails, attending unproductive meetings, dealing with interruptions, and incessantly checking their cell phones. The risk is that 90 percent of the day becomes reactive with no time for strategic thinking or growing the business. Those with a leader's mindset, on the other hand, work *on* the business as much as *in* the business.

My own poll of 1,000 leaders highlighted that 75 percent of respondents agreed with the statement "I am constantly overloaded." When we operate at such a high level of intensity for too long, we run the risk of running our mental and emotional reserves into the red. It's like a ticking time bomb. The brain floods the body with chemicals such as cortisol and noradrenaline. Primitive instincts take over, forcing the brain into fight-flight or freeze behaviors, what the eminent psychologist Dr. Steve Peters calls the "inner chimp". For a leader, this can erode objectivity and strategic perspective—essential qualities to maintain for a leader's mindset.

Daniel Goleman, in his insightful book *Focus: The Hidden Driver of Excellence*, outlines three types of focus for a leader: inner (self-awareness), outer (business context), and other (relationships). Inner focus is about holding a leadership mirror up to yourself. What are your strengths and blind spots? Outer focus is key for understanding the bigger picture: what forces are disrupting your industry? Other focus is about emotional intelligence and social skills, which are useful for building social capital.

### Use Marginal Gains

Marginal gains have been used to good effect by the Sky British cycling team to become a force in the competitive world of elite cycling. In 1996 the British Cycling Federation faced insolvency, and Great Britain was ranked an embarrassing seventeenth in the world, winning just two bronze medals at the Olympics in Atlanta. By 2012, Britain was ranked number 1 in the world, and British riders won twelve medals (eight of them gold) at the 2012 Olympic Games in London.

Sir Dave Brailsford is credited as one of the principal architects in transforming Great Britain's track fortunes over the last decade. In 2009, he was appointed the performance director and general manager of a new professional British road cycling team, Team Sky, which aimed to create the first British winner of the Tour de France within five years.

This was achieved three times, first by Bradley Wiggins in 2012, followed by Chris Froome in 2013 and 2015. Brailsford uses an ingenious principle that all leaders can tap called the "aggregation of marginal gains". Put another way, there is a 1 percent margin for improvement in everything you do, from optimizing meetings and goal setting to releasing more energy by changing your eating habits and improving nutrition. His theory is that if you can improve every area of what you do by just 1 percent, then all the small gains will multiply to achieve a 10X improvement. It's easy to overestimate the big decisions in business and miss the power of the hundreds of small actions and tiny habits that accumulate over time. Success boils down to a critical few behaviors practiced every hour of every day.

## Say No Fast and Mean It

The word "urgent" is one of the most overused words in the English language. It forces leaders everywhere to become trapped by knee-jerk cultures that simply react rather than think. Try using a range of filters to first evaluate whether the demand is the best use of your time and talent. Effective leaders are masters at protecting their time in order to get things done. They manage expectations based on reality, not fiction, and are skilled at the art of saying no to demands that are presented as urgent but are, in fact, ill-thought-out requests that will waste their day and deplete their energy.

Non-negotiables are key, otherwise the focus is lost and you will default to busywork instead of your best work. A non-negotiable is the must-have success factor you cannot compromise on—for example, a deadline or high standards.

The fact is that everyone will always want you to react to their needs immediately and on their terms. You lose control of your day and your agenda, making it impossible to fulfill your priorities. If being productive sometimes means being selfish, so be it. Effective leaders protect their time and know the difference between a time debt and time credit.

You run a time debt when you put essential tasks off. For example, not planning will increase a time debt, which you will have to repay later in the form of extra stress and a last-minute rush. Conversely, a time credit is where you are proactive; for example, thinking ahead and preventing a small issue from becoming an emergency. Remember, if everything is a priority nothing is a priority.

## Plan Backward

A leader's mindset thinks about the future. It asks what could be in the world and is comfortable with uncertainty. Planning is like taking your mind to the gym. The best leaders prioritize and decide where they want to win first. They understand that they can't win everything. Venture capitalist John Doerr advises that: "Ideas are precious, but they're relatively easy. It's execution that's everything."[169]

This may seem obvious, but most leaders try to do too much. You have to decide what to say no to and agree to new plans only if your mind and heart say yes, but this is no easy feat when everything appears urgent.

Once this is clear, remember to plan backward:

1. Figure out what it will take to win.
2. Work back from one to where you are today.
3. Create a plan to close the gap.
4. Think of your time as money.
5. Execute objectives and key results (OKRs).

OKRs are a proven framework for getting results, popularized by Doerr, who gave it to Google. Other famous users include Oracle Corporation, LinkedIn, and Zynga. OKRs help people be clear about what is expected of them. First, start by defining three to five key objectives. Objectives should be ambitious, qualitative, time led, and actionable by the individual or team. Then, under each objective, identify a couple of key result areas. These should be concrete, quantifiable, and achievable.

Betterworks is an organization that is leading the way, using OKRs to better align people and their mindsets with the strategy of the company. Zynga CEO Mark Pincus, in a *New York Times* interview, says: "We put the whole company on that, so everyone knows their OKRs. And that is a good, uncomplicated organizing principle that keeps people focused on the three things that matter most—not the 10."[170]

## Lead Fast and Slow

Pivoting quickly between fast and slow is a universal challenge for any leader: lead too quickly and you risk burnout; take too long and you miss the best opportunities. In a *Financial Times* interview, Julian Birkinshaw, professor of strategy and entrepreneurship at London Business School, was quoted as saying: "The dominant rhetoric is of accelerated change. And because the rate of change in the outside world is perceived to be getting greater, the assumption is that we should do so on the inside, too. Sometimes this creates problems, for example email traffic for its own sake."[171]

Every leader needs both fast and slow, he adds; the problem comes when there is too much of one and not enough of the other. "There are two different speeds underlying any business but some organizations default to fast and some to slow. You have to go out of your way to change that speed."[172] To lead fast and slow, do the below:

### Lead Fast:
- Do what gets the fastest result first.
- Designate a delegation hour—have a prompt in your calendar to let go.
- Beat procrastination by starting quickly.
- Become comfortable with imperfection.
- Look for coachable moments in your day.

- Doubt kills ideas, so prototype quickly.
- Communicate often.
- Keep starting until you really start.
- Celebrate success.
- Learn faster.

**Lead Slow:**

- Listen loudly.
- Play for the long game.
- Invest in prevention.
- Earn trust daily.
- Remain objective.
- Build "alone zones" for thinking.
- Unplug—it's impossible to be creative on demand.
- Protect time.
- Take brain breaks.
- Do less, better.

## Brain Breaks

The only thing that loves change is a baby with a wet diaper. "From your brain's perspective, change means learning something new, which means creating new neural pathways. This is a complex biological process that doesn't run smoothly if you are physically and mentally exhausted," says mentor Daniel Smallwood.

Smallwood suggests the following actions:

- Know the difference between doing busy work and doing your best work.
- Improve your habits to give your brain the edge it needs to lead effectively.
- Exercise and take regular brain breaks.

Finally, don't forget to take a daily shot of action-oriented optimism. When the going gets tough, summon a positive thought and look ahead rather than dwell on the past.

## FIKA

The Swedish tradition of *fika* is about more than enjoying coffee and cake; it stands for a moment to slow down and break from the routine, a moment to be alone and disconnect from the chaos of life. Most problems can probably be solved with coffee, cake, and a good old chat. Sometimes, slow can make fast happen.

## 960 MONTHS

Let us finish where we started: 960 months is the time we have to build a leader's mindset and achieve our full potential beyond profit. It's about prioritizing purpose and a legacy that leaves the planet in a better place than before. John Wood is a pioneer who lives by this credo. Many people would have you believe that you can't change the world, especially by yourself. Not Wood, who is best described as the apostle of purpose. He is the author of the best selling book *Leaving Microsoft to Change the World* and founder of Room to Read, a nonprofit organization that is helping millions of children around the world to read and write. His awe-inspiring story began one day while he was sitting at his desk as a busy, stressed-out Microsoft executive. He wondered if it was possible to radically change your life and have a second chance no matter where you are or what you are doing.

One day after endless office meetings, conference calls, and emails, he came across some photos of the majestic snow-capped Himalayas in Nepal. He decided to embark on a trekking trip, looking for nothing more than the opportunity to escape the daily grind and get some adventure. Little did he realize it at the time, but the trek in Nepal would transform Wood's life and the lives of millions of children forever.

As Wood's Nepali trek progressed, he arrived at a tiny remote school high up in the mountains and decided to pay a visit. Smiling young children gathered around him, excited to meet a visitor for the first time. The school had more than four hundred young pupils, basic equipment, and even a library, but to Wood's astonishment, no books in it. As legend has it, the headmaster looked at Wood and asked, "If you ever return in future, perhaps you could bring some books?" One year later Wood would return to the school to fulfill his promise to the headmaster, bringing hundreds of books given by friends and family, which he strapped to the back of a noisy old yak.

When the children saw the books, their faces lit up with delight. They'd never seen books before and looked in wonder at the old pages filled with words, color, and pictures. Wood realized that his second act in life was about to begin. He said to himself that he couldn't go back to a job selling software. His trek to escape office life had now turned into an extraordinary mission to change the future for the millions of children who can't read or write.

Today, Wood continues to work tirelessly around the world raising awareness of the plight of millions of children who lack basic literacy and are robbed of a future. He has been able to tap cutting-edge work practices during his time at Microsoft (focus on results, thinking big, and moving fast) to scale swiftly and make things happen. When I had the privilege of meeting him, he told me there was still much work to be done. His core belief is that "world change starts with educated children, and if they can learn to read they can read to learn." What would happen if you followed a passion or decided to fix a problem that would benefit others rather than just chasing the money? What Wood shows is that bold goals attract bold people. He had the guts to stop doing what society expected and pursue a noble goal to change lives for the better. What we can take away from that is that you don't have to be

Bill Clinton or Nelson Mandela to change the world. Anyone can do it, and Wood is living proof of that.

## DON'T BE A SPECTATOR

The team at Red Bull Stratus is made up of the best brains in science, aerospace, medicine, and engineering. Its vision is to research human extremes and transcend human potential, something all leaders are interested in. On October 14, 2014, the valiant Austrian skydiver Felix Baumgartner ascended to more than 128,000 feet above New Mexico in a helium balloon before freefalling at supersonic speeds (Mach 1.24) back to earth. His record-breaking jump broke the sound barrier and recorded vital data for scientific and medical research.

Baumgartner urges: "Don't live life as a spectator. Always examine life. Espouse new ideas. Long for new things, constantly discovering new interests, escaping from boring routines. Engage life with enthusiasm, grasping life aggressively and squeezing from it every drop of excitement, satisfaction, and joy. The key to unleashing life's potential is attitude."[173]

We can all take inspiration from Baumgartner's superhuman achievement. He set a challenging goal and had the backbone to face down unexpected problems to succeed. Every day for more than five years, he trained hard. It's the same if you want develop the leader's mindset. You must always be "on" every day, leading, inspiring, communicating, and growing your team. The path is not easy. During the fall, Baumgartner started to spin out of control and had to think quickly to stop it—no easy feat if you're dropping at over 800 miles per hour! He says: "It's way more difficult than anything I have done before." He had to overcome countless obstacles, including fear and a severe bout of claustrophobia, which threatened to disrupt the whole mission.

## EXCELSIOR

In studying leaders who are winning in the age of disruption, there are mindsets that can be replicated: think big mindset (Future Shaper), act bold mindset (Risk Taker), and learn fast mindset (Knowledge Seeker) are the three most important ones to 10X in order to harness the leader's mindset.

We all face setbacks at some point, but perhaps in failure, like seeds buried in the ground, magic lies. Steve Jobs said it best: "Knowing you are going to die is the single best way of avoiding the trap of thinking you have something to lose. You are already naked. There is no reason not to follow your heart." In the twenty-first century, you must be the CEO of your own life: own who you are and take pride in your craft, no matter how big or small.

Many years ago, when I was a young university student, one of my professors ended each class with the Latin word *excelsior*, denoting "ever upward". I can still hear the faint echo of his voice sometimes when I am in a quiet place.

I wish you great fortune on your own leadership journey. *Excelsior!*

# THE LEADER'S MINDSET SELF-ASSESSMENT

Use The Leader's Mindset self-assessment to identify your strengths and gaps for improvement. For each mindset (think big, act bold and learn fast), score your effectiveness levels on a scale from 1 (low) to 10 (high). A score of 7 or below for each of the statements indicates a priority area for improvement.

### Think Big (Future Shaper)

1. I have a bold vision for the future.

   1   2   3   4   5   6   7   8   9   10

2. I have a clear leadership purpose.

   1   2   3   4   5   6   7   8   9   10

3. I have a personal mission statement.

   1   2   3   4   5   6   7   8   9   10

4. I display personal energy and passion.

   1    2    3    4    5    6    7    8    9    10

5. I set stretching goals.

   1    2    3    4    5    6    7    8    9    10

6. I inspire everyone to see the big picture.

   1    2    3    4    5    6    7    8    9    10

7. I build a culture of innovation.

   1    2    3    4    5    6    7    8    9    10

8. I am impatient with the status quo.

   1    2    3    4    5    6    7    8    9    10

9. I hold others to account.

   1    2    3    4    5    6    7    8    9    10

10. I understand the principles of 10X thinking.

   1    2    3    4    5    6    7    8    9    10

**(Think Big Total)** _____ **/ 10 =**

## Act Bold (Risk Taker)

1. I take creative risks.

   1    2    3    4    5    6    7    8    9    10

2. I use failure as a rapid learning tool.

   1    2    3    4    5    6    7    8    9    10

3. I operate with a strong results orientation.

   1   2   3   4   5   6   7   8   9   10

4. I prototype ideas and test them quickly.

   1   2   3   4   5   6   7   8   9   10

5. I understand VUCA.

   1   2   3   4   5   6   7   8   9   10

6. I look outside my industry for inspiration.

   1   2   3   4   5   6   7   8   9   10

7. I am resilient in the face of setbacks.

   1   2   3   4   5   6   7   8   9   10

8. I make change happen.

   1   2   3   4   5   6   7   8   9   10

9. I think like an entrepreneur.

   1   2   3   4   5   6   7   8   9   10

10. I am a bold thinker.

   1   2   3   4   5   6   7   8   9   10

**(Act Bold Total)** _____ / 10 =

## Learn Fast (Knowledge Seeker)

1. I use multiple mentors to raise my game.

   1   2   3   4   5   6   7   8   9   10

2. I am proactive at knowledge networking.

   1   2   3   4   5   6   7   8   9   10

3. I have a learning plan in place.

   1   2   3   4   5   6   7   8   9   10

4. I am passionately curious about the future.

   1   2   3   4   5   6   7   8   9   10

5. I understand the power of collective intelligence.

   1   2   3   4   5   6   7   8   9   10

6. I know my personal strengths and skill gaps.

   1   2   3   4   5   6   7   8   9   10

7. I actively seek out feedback.

   1   2   3   4   5   6   7   8   9   10

8. I focus on what really matters.

   1   2   3   4   5   6   7   8   9   10

9. I protect my time.

   1   2   3   4   5   6   7   8   9   10

10. I attend a variety of learning events outside of work.

   1   2   3   4   5   6   7   8   9   10

**(Learn Fast Total)** _____ / 10 =

# ACKNOWLEDGMENTS

This book would not have been possible without the support of friends, family, and colleagues. A big thank-you to my contributors, including the inspirational John Wood, founder of Room to Read; Doug Conant, chairman of the Kellogg Institute of Leadership and former CEO and president of Campbell Soup Company; Jeff Haden, *Inc.* magazine contributing editor and ghostwriter; Chester Elton, *New York Times*–bestselling author of *What Motivates Me*, *All In*, and *The Carrot Principle*; Dr Josh Davis, director of research and lead professor at the Neuroleadership Institute (New York) and author of *Two Awesome Hours*; Alan Rozet and Chi-Chu at MITx Entrepreneurship (Massachusetts Institute of Technology); Julia Hobshawm, OBE; Octavius Black, CEO of Mind Gym; Joel Brown, founder of Addicted to Success; Kevin Kruse, *New York Times*–bestselling author; all the team at Bottega Veneta (Milan); Emilia Lahti, mental toughness researcher and *sisu* expert; Jésus Blanco, CEO and co-founder of Linktia; Hans

Balmaekers, CEO and founder of Saam; and all the team at Future Ideas (www.futureideas.org).

I'd like to thank Leigh Kendall and his world-class team at Informa Middle East (Deeba Yunis, Nicola Bell, Anton Long, Mohamed Attia, Simon Fernandes, Lynn Hunter, Vandhana Rajput, Mharny Martinez, Riza Rabang-Pablo, Ana Malsi, and Aneel Aranha), as well as all the CEOs, delegates, and startups I've worked with over the years.

I owe a huge thank you to my editor, Amanda Rooker, and her superb team at SplitSeed; Barbara Tezler at Tezlerpr, Inc.; Corey Majeau for his superb illustrations and Morgan James Publishing (New York) for supporting the publication of this book.

Finally, I'd like to thank my best friends, Sonia Mauri, Lucia Alice Mauri, Tom Gregory, Marcello Muiesan, Matthew Ryder, Neil Connor, Michael Digby, Julian Compton, and William and Frances Welch of Studio William, for always being there.

# NOTES

## CHAPTER 1: UNLOCKING THE LEADER'S MINDSET

1   Susan Johnston, "Expert Advice on How to Build the Ultimate To-Do List", *Fast Company*, April 15, 2015, http://www.fastcompany.com/3044945/work-smart/expert-advice-on-how-to-build-the-ultimate-to-do-list.

2   Ben Spencer, "Mobile Users Can't Leave Their Phone Alone for Six Minutes and Check It up to 150 Times a Day", *Daily Mail*, February 10, 2013, http://www.dailymail.co.uk/news/article-2276752/Mobile-users-leave-phone-minutes-check-150-times-day.html.

3   H. A. Simon, "Designing Organizations for an Information-Rich World", in *Computers, Communication, and the Public Interest*, ed. Martin Greenberger (Baltimore: Johns Hopkins Press, 1971), 40–41.

4   Niall McCarthy, "Enslaved by Your Alarm Clock? Only One in Seven Americans Wake up Feeling Fresh Every Day [Infographic]", *Forbes*, June 4, 2015, http://www.forbes.com/sites/niallmccarthy/2015/06/04/enslaved-by-your-alarm-clock-only-1-in-7-americans-wake-up-feeling-fresh-every-day-infographic.

5   "400 Million Stories", WhatsApp blog, December 19, 2013, https://blog.whatsapp.com/472/400-Million-Stories.

6   Zoe Wood, "Facebook Turned Down WhatsApp Co-Founder Brian Acton for Job in 2009", *Guardian*, February 20, 2014, http://www.theguardian.com/technology/2014/feb/20/facebook-turned-down-whatsapp-co-founder-brian-acton-job-2009.

7   Chris Smith, "WhatsApp Exists Thanks to Twitter and Facebook's Ignorance", Yahoo! News, February 20, 2014, http://news.yahoo.com/whatsapp-exists-thanks-twitter-facebook-ignorance-194121524.html.

8   Brian Acton, Twitter post, August 3, 2009, 12:14 pm, https://twitter.com/brianacton/status/3109544383.

9   J. J. Colao, "At $19 Billion, WhatsApp Is Worth More than Under Armour, Xerox and These Other Storied Brands", *Forbes*, February 19, 2014, http://www.forbes.com/sites/jjcolao/2014/02/19/at-19-billion-whatsapp-is-worth-more-than-under-armour-xerox-and-these-other-storied-brands.

10  Ibid.

11  David Rowan, "Astro Teller of Google[x] Wants to Improve the World's Broken Industries", Wired.co.uk, October 31, 2013, http://www.wired.co.uk/magazine/archive/2013/11/start/destination-moon.

12  Carolyn E. Tajnai, "Fred Terman: The Father of Silicon Valley". Paper presented at the Stanford Computer Forum, Stanford

University, Stanford, CA, May 1985, http://forum.stanford.edu/carolyn/terman.

13 Erin Griffith and Dan Primack, "The Age of Unicorns", *Fortune*, January 22, 2015, http://fortune.com/2015/01/22/the-age-of-unicorns.

14 Denise Delahanty, "Factory Workers Don't Care about Their Company's Mission", Gallup, January 16, 2015, http://www.gallup.com/businessjournal/181175/factory-workers-don-care-company-mission.aspx.

15 Robert Safian, "Generation Flux's Secret Weapon", *Fast Company*, November 2014, http://www.fastcompany.com/3035975/generation-flux/find-your-mission.

16 Emilia Lahti, "The Brilliance of a Dream: Introducing the Action Mindset", Creativity Post, December 2, 2013, http://www.creativitypost.com/psychology/the_brilliance_of_a_dream_introducing_the_action_mindset.

17 "The Science of Hope: An Interview with Shane Lopez", Taking Charge of Your Health and Wellbeing, University of Minnesota, http://www.takingcharge.csh.umn.edu/article/05-2013/science-hope-interview-shane-lopez.

18 Yves Morieux, "As Work Gets More Complex, 6 Rules to Simplify", TED, October 2013, https://www.ted.com/talks/yves_morieux_as_work_gets_more_complex_6_rules_to_simplify.

19 Emma Jacobs, "'Smartcuts' Advocates Adopting a Hacker Mind-Set for Speedy Success", *Los Angeles Times*, September 21, 2014, http://www.latimes.com/business/la-fi-books-20140921-story.html.

20 Smiley Poswolsky, "Quarter-Life Breakthroughs, Not Crises, for the Purpose Generation", *Good*, July 24, 2013, http://magazine.

good.is/articles/quarter-life-breakthroughs-not-crises-for-the-purpose-generation.

21    Lord Byron, "Extracts from Don Juan: Haidée and Juan", *The English Poets*, vol. 4, ed. Thomas Humphry Ward, http://www.bartleby.com/337/995.html.

22    Michael V. Copeland, "Resiliency, Risk, and a Good Compass: Tools for the Coming Chaos" [interview with Joi Ito], *Wired*, June 11, 2012, http://www.wired.com/2012/06/resiliency-risk-and-a-good-compass-how-to-survive-the-coming-chaos.

## CHAPTER 2: THINK BIG (FUTURE SHAPER)

23    Emilia Lahti, "The Brilliance of a Dream: Introducing the Action Mindset", Creativity Post, December 2, 2013, http://www.creativitypost.com/psychology/the_brilliance_of_a_dream_introducing_the_action_mindset.

24    "The 100 Richest Tech Billionaires from around the Globe", *Forbes*, August 5, 2015, http://www.forbes.com/profile/elon-musk.

25    Chris Anderson, "Elon Musk's Mission to Mars", *Wired*, October 21, 2012, http://www.wired.com/2012/10/ff-elon-musk-qa.

26    Doug Gross, "The CNN 10: Thinkers: Elon Musk", CNN, http://edition.cnn.com/interactive/2013/10/tech/cnn10-thinkers.

27    Wikipedia, s.v. "Elon Musk", http://en.wikipedia.org/wiki/Elon_Musk, accessed May 17, 2015.

28    Drake Baer, "22 Quotes That Take You Inside Elon Musk's Brilliant, Eccentric Mind", *Business Insider*, June 19, 2014, http://www.businessinsider.com/brilliant-elon-musk-quotes-2014-6.

29    Elon Musk, AZ Quotes, http://www.azquotes.com/
      quote/779436, accessed October 1, 2015.

30    Elon Musk, "Magicians of the 21st Century", commencement
      address, Caltech, June 15, 2012, http://commencement.caltech.
      edu/archive/speakers/2012_address.

31    Alex Davies, "These Dreamers Are Actually Making Progress
      Building Elon's Hyperloop", *Wired*, December 19, 2014, http://
      www.wired.com/2014/12/jumpstartfund-hyperloop-elon-musk.

32    2015 Tesla Model S report, *Consumer Reports*, http://www.
      consumerreports.org/cro/tesla-model-s.htm, accessed October 1,
      2015.

33    Doug Gross, "The CNN 10: Thinkers: Elon Musk", CNN,
      http://edition.cnn.com/interactive/2013/10/tech/cnn10-
      thinkers.

34    Drake Baer, "22 Quotes That Take You Inside Elon Musk's
      Brilliant, Eccentric Mind", *Business Insider*, June 19, 2014,
      http://www.businessinsider.com/brilliant-elon-musk-
      quotes-2014-6.

35    Sheryl Sandberg, "Sheryl Sandberg Addresses the Class of 2012",
      Harvard Business School Speech, May 23, 2012, https://www.
      youtube.com/watch?v=2Db0_RafutM.

36    Juro Osawa, Gillian Wong, and Rick Carew, "Xiaomi Becomes
      World's Most Valuable Tech Startup", *Wall Street Journal*,
      December 29, 2014, http://www.wsj.com/articles/xiaomi-
      becomes-worlds-most-valuable-tech-startup-1419843430.

37    "When Workers Are Owners", *Economist*, August 22, 2015,
      http://www.economist.com/news/business/21661657-received-
      wisdom-employee-ownership-good-thing-comes-caveats-when-
      workers-are.

38    Daniel Burrus, "Being Big Is No Longer Enough; Today the
      Fast Eat the Slow", *Huffington Post*, February 11, 2013, http://

www.huffingtonpost.com/daniel-burrus/being-big-is-no-longer-en_b_2286194.html.

39    Richard Wachman, "Blockbuster Files for Chapter 11 Protection", *Guardian*, September 23, 2010, http://www.theguardian.com/business/2010/sep/23/blockbuster-chapter-11.

40    Peter Tufano, "The Ripple Effect", *Financial Times*, March 20, 2015, http://www.ft.com/intl/cms/s/2/39b4a466-c5f1-11e4-ab8f-00144feab7de.html#axzz3nKdhrhjO.

41    Kieron Monks, "How CEOs Predict the Future", CNN, January 28, 2015, http://www.cnn.com/2015/01/28/world/ceos-predict-future.

42    Omar Ismail, "*Where Good Ideas Come From*, by Steven Johnson, a Reflection, Week 7", Medium, February 11, 2014, http://medium.com/52-book-year/where-good-ideas-come-from-by-steven-johnson-2000216ec0d8.

43    "Leadership Words to Live By", Conant Leadership, http://conantleadership.com/leadership-words-to-live-by, accessed October 1, 2015.

44    Amy Cosper, "Why Entrepreneurs Are Shepherds of Renaissance", *Entrepreneur*, April 21, 2015, http://www.entrepreneur.com/article/244482.

45    Wikipedia, s.v. "The Hedgehog and the Fox", https://en.wikipedia.org/wiki/The_Hedgehog_and_the_Fox, accessed July 5, 2015.

46    "Our Story", Nokia, http://company.nokia.com/en/about-us/our-company/our-story, accessed October 1, 2015.

47    "The Best 100 Brands: Previous Years, 2005", Interbrand, http://bestglobalbrands.com/previous-years/2005, accessed October 1, 2015.

48    "Curtain Falls on Nokia's Finnish Home in Boom-to-Bust Demise", *BusinessWorld*, July 9, 2015, http://www.bworldonline.

com/content.php?section=Corporate&title=curtain-falls-on-nokias-finnish-home-in-boom-to-bust-demise&id=111241.

49 Natasha Lomas, "Microsoft's $7.2BN+ Acquisition of Nokia's Devices Business Is Now Complete", TechCrunch, April 25, 2014, http://techcrunch.com/2014/04/25/microsofts-7-2bn-acquisition-of-nokias-devices-business-is-now-complete.

50 Dominic Rushe and Sam Theilman, "Google to Restructure into New Holding Company Called Alphabet", Guardian, August 11, 2015, http://www.theguardian.com/technology/2015/aug/10/google-alphabet-parent-company.

51 Harvard Business Review Staff, "The Best Performing CEOs in the World", Harvard Business Review, November 2014, https://hbr.org/2014/11/the-best-performing-ceos-in-the-world.

52 Steven Levy, "Jeff Bezos Owns the Web in More Ways than You Think", Wired, November 13, 2011, http://www.wired.com/2011/11/ff_bezos.

53 Sean Hassall, "The Psychology of Hope" [review of The Psychology of Hope, by C. R. Snyder], September 25, 2011, http://seanhassall.com/2011/09/25/the-psychology-of-hope.

54 Nick Craig and Scott A. Snook, "From Purpose to Impact", Harvard Business Review, May 2014, https://hbr.org/2014/05/from-purpose-to-impact.

55 Ibid.

56 Laszlo Bock, Work Rules: Insights from Inside Google That Will Transform How You Live and Lead (New York: Twelve, 2015), 40.

57 "Letter from the CEO", PepsiCo website, https://www.pepsico.com/Purpose/Performance-with-Purpose/Letter-from-the-CEO, accessed October 1, 2015.

58 Amazon.com Facebook page, https://www.facebook.com/Amazon/info?tab=page_info, accessed October 1, 2015.

59    Jeffery P. Bezos, 1997 letter to shareholders, http://media. corporate-ir.net/media_files/irol/97/97664/reports/ Shareholderletter97.pdf.

60    Rik Kirkland, "Wharton's Adam Grant on the Key to Professional Success", June 2014, http://www.mckinsey.com/ insights/organization/whartons_adam_grant_on_the_key_to_ professional_success.

61    "Company Info", Facebook.com, https://newsroom.fb.com/ company-info, accessed October 1, 2015.

62    Zach Bulygo, "Entrepreneurial Lessons from Mark Zuckerberg", Kissmetrics, February 2013, https://blog.kissmetrics.com/ lessons-from-mark-zuckerberg/.

63    Yvo M. C. Meevissen, Madelon L. Peters, and Hugo J. E. M. Alberts, "Become More Optimistic by Imagining a Best Possible Self: Effects of a Two Week Intervention", *Journal of Behavior Therapy and Experimental Psychiatry* 42 (2011): 371–378.

64    Karen X. Cheng, "Dance Dance Revelation: Viral Star Karen X. Cheng on How to Have More Discipline", *Fast Company*, July 23, 2013, http://www.fastcompany.com/3014652/dance-dance-revelation-viral-star-karen-x-cheng-on-how-to-have-more-discipline.

65    "Big Demands and High Expectations: The Deloitte Millennial Survey", executive summary, Deloitte, January 2014, http:// www2.deloitte.com/content/dam/Deloitte/global/Documents/ About-Deloitte/2014_MillennialSurvey_ExecutiveSummary_ FINAL.pdf.

66    Rick Tetzeli and Brent Schlender, "Tim Cook on Apple's Future: Everything Can Change Except Values", *Fast Company*, April 2015, http://www.fastcompany.com/3042435/steves-legacy-tim-looks-ahead.

67    Marc Benioff and Carlye Adler, *Behind the Cloud: The Untold Story of How Salesforce.com Went from Idea to Billion-Dollar Company—and Revolutionized an Industry* (San Francisco: Jossey-Bass, 2009), 16.

68    Ryan Mac, "Five Startup Lessons from GoPro Founder and Billionaire Nick Woodman", *Forbes*, March 13, 2013, http://www.forbes.com/sites/ryanmac/2013/03/13/five-startup-lessons-from-gopro-founder-and-billionaire-nick-woodman.

69    Richard Branson, Twitter post, July 15, 2015, https://twitter.com/richardbranson/status/621421723909521408.

70    GoPro home page, http://gopro.madison.co.uk/#sthash.ph6y4pGS.dpuf.

71    Gavin Brett, "How GoPro Cameras Have Made Nothing Unfilmable, by the Man Who Created Them", *Telegraph*, February 28, 2015, http://www.telegraph.co.uk/technology/11434321/How-GoPro-cameras-have-made-nothing-unfilmable-by-the-man-who-invented-them.html.

72    Sam Moulton, "GoPro Founder Nick Woodman: 'I Am Doing This'", *Outside*, September 18, 2013, http://www.outsideonline.com/1870296/gopro-founder-nick-woodman-i-am-doing.

73    Gavin Brett, "How GoPro Cameras Have Made Nothing Unfilmable, by the Man Who Created Them", *Telegraph*, February 28, 2015, http://www.telegraph.co.uk/technology/11434321/How-GoPro-cameras-have-made-nothing-unfilmable-by-the-man-who-invented-them.html.

74    "The 100 Richest Tech Billionaires from around the Globe", *Forbes*, August 5, 2015, http://www.forbes.com/profile/nicholas-woodman/?list=forbes-400.

75    Woodman, Nick, "GoPro CEO Nicholas Woodman Discusses Inspiration, Disrupt SF 2013", YouTube video, interview by

Matt Burns, September 11, 2013, https://www.youtube.com/watch?v=l9-Q0Kboro4.

76 Ryan Mac, "The Mad Billionaire behind GoPro: The World's Hottest Camera Company", *Forbes*, March 4, 2013, http://www.forbes.com/sites/ryanmac/2013/03/04/the-mad-billionaire-behind-gopro-the-worlds-hottest-camera-company.

77 "Your Employees Are Not Mind Readers" by Douglas R. Conant, January 4, 2013, https://hbr.org/2013/01/your-employees-are-not-mind-re, accessed October 8, 2015

## CHAPTER 3: ACT BOLD (RISK TAKER)

78 "The Ten Most Innovative Companies in Asia", *Forbes*, http://www.forbes.com/pictures/eghe45edmjm/2-rakuten-japan, accessed August 14, 2015.

79 "English Speaking Japanese Companies", GaijinPot, June 30, 2010, http://injapan.gaijinpot.com/work/starting-a-business-work/2010/06/30/english-speaking-japanese-companies.

80 Shu, Catherine, "Japanese Internet Giant Rakuten Acquires Viber for $900M", TechCrunch, February 13, 2014, http://techcrunch.com/2014/02/13/japanese-internet-giant-rakuten-acquires-viber-for-900m/.

81 Andrey Gidaspov, "Risk Averse? Scared to Pilot a New Project? Learn the 3rd Principle of Rakuten", Giadaspov.com, October 12, 2013, http://gidaspov.com/2013/10/12/diving-horse.

82 Hiroshi Mikitani, *Marketplace 3.0: Rewriting the Rules of Borderless Business* (New York: Palgrave, 2013), 1.

83 Parmy Olson and Tomio Geron, "Mission Impossible: How Rakuten Billionaire Hiroshi Mikitani Plans to 'Beat Amazon'", *Forbes*, September 6, 2012, http://www.forbes.com/sites/parmyolson/2012/09/06/mission-impossible-how-rakuten-billionaire-hiroshi-mikitani-plans-to-beat-amazon.

84 Hiroshi Mikitani, "Hiroshi Mikitani: 'Marketplace 3.0': Talks at Google", YouTube video, interview by Daniel Alegre, April 8, 2013, https://www.youtube.com/watch?v=xI-820hpFxg.

85 Wikipedia, s.v. "Lean Manufacturing", https://en.wikipedia.org/wiki/Lean_manufacturing, accessed August 15, 2015.

86 Hiroshi Mikitani, *Marketplace 3.0: Rewriting the Rules of Borderless Business* (New York: Palgrave, 2013), 107.

87 Hiroshi Mikitani, "You Can Do Better", LinkedIn Pulse, June 20, 2013, https://www.linkedin.com/pulse/20130620134755-52782505-you-can-do-better.

88 Ed O'Boyle and Jim Harter, "State of the American Manager: Analytics and Advice for Leaders", Gallup, 2013, http://www.gallup.com/services/182138/state-american-manager.aspx.

89 Hiroshi Mikitani, *Marketplace 3.0: Rewriting the Rules of Borderless Business* (New York: Palgrave, 2013), 114.

90 Ibid., 118.

91 Ibid., 125.

92 "BCG Technology Advantage", Boston Consulting Group, http://media-publications.bcg.com/BCG_Technology_Advantage_April_2015.pdf, 4.

93 "The Entrepreneur Inside", EY, http://ukcareers.ey.com/experienced/the-entrepreneur-inside.

94 Paul Graham, "Schlep Blindness", January 2012, http://www.paulgraham.com/schlep.

95 Paul Graham, "How to Get Startup Ideas", November 2012, www.paulgraham.com/startupideas.

96 Josh Linkner, "Think Like a Startup", *Forbes*, April 16, 2012, http://www.forbes.com/sites/joshlinkner/2012/04/16/think-like-a-startup.

97 "Recruiter Spotlight: Cody, This Week's @InsideZappos Social VIP", Zappos blog, http://blogs.zappos.com/blogs/zappos-

family/2014/08/08/recruiter-spotlight-cody-weeks-insidezappos-social-vip.

98   "Mark Randall" [biography], Lean Startup Conference, November 17, 2014, http://2014.leanstartup.co/oospeaker/mark-randall.

99   Ibid.

100  Ed Catmull, "How Pixar Fosters Creativity", *Harvard Business Review*, September 2008, https://hbr.org/2008/09/how-pixar-fosters-collective-creativity.

101  Ibid.

102  Emilia Lahti, "The Brilliance of a Dream: Introducing the Action Mindset", Creativity Post, December 2, 2013, http://www.creativitypost.com/psychology/the_brilliance_of_a_dream_introducing_the_action_mindset.

103  J. K. Rowling, "Text of J. K. Rowling's Speech: 'The Fringe Benefits of Failure, and the Importance of Imagination'", Harvard Gazette, June 5, 2008, http://news.harvard.edu/gazette/story/2008/06/text-of-j-k-rowling-speech.

104  FailCon, http://www.thefailcon.com/about.html, accessed October 1, 2015.

105  D. Anthony Storm's Commentary on Kierkegaard, www.sorenkierkegaard.org, acccessed August 28, 2015.

106  Marina Krakovsky, "The Effort Effect", *Stanford Alumni*, March/April 2007, https://alumni.stanford.edu/get/page/magazine/article/?article_id=32124.

107  Mezon Almellehan, "The 100 Most Influential People: Malala Yousafzai", *Time*, April 16, 2015, http://time.com/3822637/malala-yousafzai-2015-time-100.

108  Janina Marguc, Jens Förster, and Gerben A. Van Kleef, "Stepping Back to See the Big Picture: When Obstacles Elicit

Global Processing", *Journal of Personality and Social Psychology* 101, no. 5 (2011), 883–901.

109 "Dropbox", *Forbes*, October 19, 2011, http://www.forbes.com/forbes/2011/1107/best-companies-11-drew-houston-steve-jobs-ferdowsi-dropbox-barret.html.

110 "Who We Are, What We Stand For", Airbnb website, http://blog.airbnb.com/who-we-are.

111 Marcus Aurelius, *Meditations*.

112 "FailCon 2011: Uber Case Study", YouTube video, November 3, 2011, https://youtu.be/2QrX5jsiico.

113 Ibid.

114 Richard Feloni, "How Uber CEO Travis Kalanick Went from a Startup Failure to One of the Hottest Names in Silicon Valley", *Business Insider*, September 24, 2014, http://www.businessinsider.com/uber-ceo-travis-kalanicks-success-story-2014-9.

115 Travis Kalanick, Startup Quotes, http://startuptxt.com/22-travis-kalanick-about-fear.

116 "FailCon 2011: Uber Case Study", YouTube video, November 3, 2011, https://youtu.be/2QrX5jsiico.

117 Al Ramadan, Christopher Lochhead, and Dave Peterson, "Behind Uber's Soaring Value", *Fortune*, December 11, 2014, http://fortune.com/2014/12/11/behind-ubers-soaring-value/.

118 Carol Ross Joynt, "A Q&A with Travis Kalanick, CEO of Uber", *Washingtonian*, January 11, 2012, http://www.washingtonian.com/blogs/capitalcomment/power-players/a-qa-with-travis-kalanick-ceo-of-uber.php.

119 "FailCon 2011: Uber Case Study", YouTube video, November 3, 2011, https://youtu.be/2QrX5jsiico.

120 Jerry Zucker, "Address by Jerry Zucker" [commencement address], *University of Wisconsin–Madison News*, May 20, 2003, http://news.wisc.edu/8682.

121 Michael V. Copeland, "Resiliency, Risk, and a Good Compass: Tools for the Coming Chaos" [interview with Joi Ito], *Wired*, June 11, 2012, http://www.wired.com/2012/06/resiliency-risk-and-a-good-compass-how-to-survive-the-coming-chaos.

122 Vivian Giang, "11 Famous Entrepreneurs Share How They Overcame Their Biggest Failure", *Fast Company*, May 1, 2014, http://www.fastcompany.com/3029883/bottom-line/11-famous-entrepreneurs-share-how-they-overcame-their-biggest-failure.

123 Josephine Moulds, "Failure? There's No Better Way to Make a Success of Yourself", *The Times*, May 25, 2015, http://www.thetimes.co.uk/tto/business/workinglife/article4449942.ece.

124 Kiki Loizou, "Coffee's Ready: £4M Injection for Delivery Start-Up", *Sunday Times*, January 25, 2015, http://www.thesundaytimes.co.uk/sto/business/Retail_and_leisure/article1511071.ece.

125 Phil Hansen, "Embrace the Shake", TED talk, February 2013, https://www.ted.com/talks/phil_hansen_embrace_the_shake.

## CHAPTER 4: LEARN FAST (KNOWLEDGE SEEKER)

126 Albert Bandura, "The Psychology of Chance Encounters and Life Events", *American Psychologist*, vol. 37, no. 7 (1982), http://www.itari.in/categories/higherpurpose/psychology_of_life.pdf.

127 David Kirkpatrick, "With a Little Help from His Friends", *Vanity Fair*, October 2010, http://www.vanityfair.com/culture/2010/10/sean-parker-201010.

128 Paul Graham, "Why Startup Hubs Work", October 2011, http://www.paulgraham.com/hubs.html.

129 Samuel Arbesman, *The Half-Life of Facts: Why Everything We Know Has an Expiration Date* (New York: Current, 2012), 2–3.

130 Ibid., 7.

131 Margaret Heffernan, *Beyond Measure: The Big Impact of Small Changes* (New York: TED Books, 2015), 23.

132 Zoe Williams, "Julia Hobsbawm: 'I'm Interested in Social Mobility, and I Think There Is a Stuckness Going On'", *Guardian*, October 10, 2014, http://www.theguardian.com/society/2014/oct/10/julia-hobsbawm-queen-of-networking.

133 Sam Altman, "Why Silicon Valley Works", November 3, 2014, http://blog.samaltman.com/why-silicon-valley-works.

134 Matthew D. Lieberman, *Social: Why Our Brains Are Wired to Connect* (New York: Crown, 2013), 10.

135 Rik Kirkland, "Wharton's Adam Grant on the Key to Professional Success", June 2014, http://www.mckinsey.com/insights/organization/whartons_adam_grant_on_the_key_to_professional_success.

136 Morten Hansen, *Collaboration: How Leaders Avoid the Traps, Build Common Ground, and Reap Big Results* (Boston: Harvard Business School Publishing, 2009), 127.

137 Michael Simmons, "The No. 1 Predictor of Career Success According to Network Science", *Forbes*, January 15, 2015, http://www.forbes.com/sites/michaelsimmons/2015/01/15/this-is-the-1-predictor-of-career-success-according-to-network-science/2.

138 Eric Schmidt and Jonathan Rosenberg with Alan Eagle, *How Google Works: The Rules for Success in the Internet Century* (New York: Grand Central, 2014), 40.

139 Wikipedia, s.v. "Asch Conformity Experiments", https://en.wikipedia.org/wiki/Asch_conformity_experiments, accessed October 1, 2015.

140 Aleks Krotoski, "Robin Dunbar: We Can Only Ever Have 150 Friends at Most…" *Guardian*, March 13, 2010, http://www.theguardian.com/technology/2010/mar/14/my-bright-idea-robin-dunbar.

141 "Drew Houston's Commencement Address", MIT News, http://news.mit.edu/2013/commencement-address-houston-0607.

142 Gary Wolf, "Steve Jobs: The Next Insanely Great Thing", *Wired*, February 1996, http://archive.wired.com/wired/archive/4.02/jobs_pr.html.

143 Alex Konrad, "Here's All the VC Firms Who Made More on the Box IPO than Its CEO", *Forbes*, January 23, 2015, http://www.forbes.com/sites/alexkonrad/2015/01/23/all-the-vc-firms-who-made-more-on-the-box-ipo-than-its-ceo.

144 Nick Statt, "Box CEO Aaron Levie on Finding Mentors and Mixing Enterprise/Consumer Cultures", Readwrite, February 20, 2013, http://readwrite.com/2013/02/20/box-ceo-aaron-levie-on-seeking-out-mentors-mixing-enterprise-consumer-cultures-video.

145 Aditya Maheshwari, "Who Mentored Mark Zuckerberg?", Mentii, June 13, 2013, https://mentii.com/blog/who-mentored-mark-zuckerberg-.html.

146 Andrea Huspeni, "Meet Behind-the-Scenes Mentors of 15 Top Tech Executives", *Business Insider*, July 11, 2012, http://www.businessinsider.com/meet-the-mentors-behind-the-visionaries-of-tech-2012-7.

147 Nicole Perlroth, "15 Minutes With: Reid Hoffman, The Guru", Forbes, April 6, 2011, http://www.forbes.com/sites/nicoleperlroth/2011/04/06/15-minutes-with-reid-hoffman-theguru.

148 "About", MIT Center for Collective Intelligence website, http://cci.mit.edu/about_mitcenter.html, accessed April 11, 2016.

149 Anita Woolley, Thomas W. Malone, and Christopher Chabris, "Gray Matter: Why Some Teams Are Smarter than Others", *New York Times*, January 16, 2015, http://www.nytimes. com/2015/01/18/opinion/sunday/why-some-teams-are-smarter-than-others.html.

150 Matthew Syed, "Exclusive: 'Spa Was the Defining Moment. We Knew That Internal Rivalry Can Destroy Teams'", *The Times*, November 25, 2014, http://www.thetimes.co.uk/tto/sport/formulaone/article4277331.ece.

151 "Create a Team with Complementary Strengths", Stanford Graduate School of Business, http://stanfordbusiness.tumblr. com/post/121850561639/create-a-team-with-complementary-strengths, accessed October 1, 2015.

152 Julie Bort, "At 27, This Guy Quit a $500,000 Job at BlackBerry to Launch a Cool Startup", *Business Insider*, February 16, 2015, http://businessinsider.com/this-guy-left-a-500k-job-for-a-startup-2015-2.

153 Bob Morris, "Liz Wiseman: Part 2 of an Interview by Bob Morris", Blogging on Business, April 8, 2015, http://bobmorris. biz/liz-wiseman-part-2-of-an-interview-by-bob-morris.

154 Evelyn Diaz, "Doreetha Daniels Gets College Degree at Age 99", BET, June 6, 2015, http://www.bet.com/news/national/2015/06/06/doreetha-daniels-99-fulfills-dream-of-graduating-college.html.

**CHAPTER 5: FINAL THOUGHTS, HACKS, AND SHORTCUTS**

155 Seelig, Tina, *What I Wish I Knew When I Was 20: A Crash Course on Making Your Place in the World* (New York: HarperOne, 2011), 126.

156 Steve Jobs, "'You've Got to Find What You Love,' Jobs Says" [commencement address transcript], Stanford News, June 14,

2005, http://news.stanford.edu/news/2005/june15/jobs-061505.
html.

157 Richard Wiseman, "Be Lucky: It's an Easy Skill to Learn",
*Telegraph*, January 9, 2003, http://www.telegraph.co.uk/
technology/3304496/Be-lucky-its-an-easy-skill-to-learn.html.

158 Richard Wiseman, "The Luck Factor", *Skeptical Inquirer*, May/
June 2013, 2, http://richardwiseman.com/resources/The_Luck_
Factor.pdf.

159 Ibid., 3.

160 Richard Wiseman, "Be Lucky: It's an Easy Skill to Learn",
*Telegraph*, January 9, 2003, http://www.telegraph.co.uk/
technology/3304496/Be-lucky-its-an-easy-skill-to-learn.html.

161 Ibid.

162 Albert Szent-Györgyi, Brainy Quote, http://www.brainyquote.
com/quotes/quotes/a/albertszen126437.html.

163 Sahar Hashemi, "What Makes an Entrepreneur?" YouTube
video, November 12, 2014, https://www.youtube.com/
watch?v=r8nHptyS234.

164 Sahar Hashemi, "Eight Habits", http://saharhashemi.com/eight-
habits-3.

165 Ibid.

166 Ibid.

167 Sahar Hashemi, "Switching on the Entrepreneurial Mindset",
IMD, May 30, 2014, http://www.imd.org/news/Switching-on-
the-entrepreneurial-mindset.cfm.

168 Adam B. Blake, Meenely Nazarian, and Alan D. Castel, "The
Apple of the Mind's Eye: Everyday Attention, Metamemory,
and Reconstructive Memory for the Apple Logo", *Quarterly
Journal of Experimental Psychology* 68, no. 5 (2015), http://www.
tandfonline.com/doi/full/10.1080/17470218.2014.1002798#.
VeYRUx3H8aI.

169 Alex Moffit, "John Doerr on OKRs and Goal Setting at Google and Intel", Social Media Today, September 4, 2014, http://www.socialmediatoday.com/content/john-doerr-okrs-and-goal-setting-google-and-intel-video.

170 Adam Bryant, "Are You a C.E.O. of Something?" [interview with Mark Pincus], New York Times, January 30, 2010, http://www.nytimes.com/2010/01/31/business/31corner.html.

171 Emma De Vita, "Managing Fast and Slow in a World That Keeps Accelerating", Financial Times, January 14, 2015, http://www.ft.com/cms/s/0/30aa29f0-9a5d-11e4-8426-00144feabdc0.html#axzz3gWSlsX8n.

172 Ibid.

173 Felix Baumgartner, Goodreads, http://www.goodreads.com/author/quotes/6556063.Felix_Baumgartner.

# About the Author

Terence Mauri is an author, keynote speaker, mentor and advisor to some of the world's most successful companies. He has been recognized as an *Inc.* magazine Top 100 Leadership Expert and Top 100 Leadership Thinker to follow on Twitter (@terencemauri).

Terence serves as a mentor for Future Ideas (www.futureideas.org), an international panel of experts that includes some of the world's biggest thinkers, such as Dan Pink (Drive), Richard Florida (Rotman School, University of Toronto), and Rita McGrath (associate professor at the Columbia University Graduate School of Business). He is also a lead host for 9others.com, a thriving forum for connecting entrepreneurs around the world.

You can reach Terence Mauri at www.terencemauri.com.

CPSIA information can be obtained
at www.ICGtesting.com
Printed in the USA
FSHW010459090921
84650FS